1 MONTH OF
FREE
READING

at

www.ForgottenBooks.com

By purchasing this book you are eligible for one month membership to ForgottenBooks.com, giving you unlimited access to our entire collection of over 1,000,000 titles via our web site and mobile apps.

To claim your free month visit:
www.forgottenbooks.com/free1126956

ISBN 978-0-331-45851-0
PIBN 11126956

Contents

Dedication 7

President's Message 9

Faculty 13

Seniors 27

Classes 87

Features 111

Organizations 129

Athletics 163

Directories 173

Dedication

To

MARIE BADGER

Teacher and Friend

We Dedicate

With Affection and Respect

THE CLIPPER OF 1940

The President's Message

The optimist believes that reality is essentially good. He sees life as a glorious adventure full of thrilling experiences and the pursuit of exciting ideals. Disappointment, defeat, frustration and kindred reverses are to him only stimuli toward the realization of happiness and the accomplishment of worthwhile things.

The pessimist is a misanthrope whose world holds nothing but a vast potpourri of shattered illusions and broken dreams. He subscribes with Schopenhauer to the monstrous teaching that misery and failure are the natural state of man. To him the past offers no inspiration; the future, no hope.

Somewhere between these divergent philosophies lies the true perspective. Life is not exclusively either joyful or sorrowful. It is a medley of many tunes. That man gets most out of life who successfully harmonizes the greatest number of notes. Most of us have difficulty in attaining this objective because discouragements usually multiply with the passing years. Youth is a time of brave ambition and high resolve. Maturity is a test of courage and will. Too many of us go down into the shadows and have not strength enough to dissipate the enveloping gloom.

The garlands belong to those who find the sun. Tennyson expressed this truth perfectly when he wrote:

"I hold it truth with him who sings
To one clear harp in diverse tones
That men may rise on stepping stones
Of their dead selves to higher things."

You seniors stand at the portcullis of life. Behind you are roads which have been not too torturous. You have come a long way with comparatively few unpleasant experiences. Possibly your troubles have been magnified for a time, but the buoyancy of youth has served you in good stead to preserve optimism and intensify faith. Before you lurk your enemies. They are the same implacable foes whom we all have to fight. They are fully armed and they know no fear. Bunyan tells about them in "Pilgrim's Progress". They have been campaigning for centuries behind the same red moat.

This is not a professional exhortation. We are not concerned so much with your success as teachers—we are interested in your success as men and women. Despite a popular misconception, nearly all of our graduates eventually find their niche and build auspiciously on the foundations laid in the classrooms at Salem. I hope we may be able to say in the years to come that you have been good warriors too, that you have fought with the tenacity which characterized your earlier struggles, that you have never lost sight of the standard-bearer in the vanguard—that you have marched in a solid phalanx to the victory of our dreams.

EDWARD A. SULLIVAN

II

Faculty

College Faculty

CHARLES ELMER DONER
Handwriting

GERTRUDE BROWN GOLDSMITH
A. B., A. M.
Biological Science

VERNA BELLE FLANDERS
B. S., S. M.
Geography

WALTER GEORGE WHITMAN
A. B., A. M.
Physical Science

ALEXANDER HUGH SPROUL
S. B., S. M.
Business Education

MARIE BADGER, B. S. ED.
Typewriting, Speech

FLORENCE BARNES CRUTTENDEN
B. S., M. A.
History, Economics, Sociology

MAUDE LYMAN HARRIS
A. B., A. M.
Literature, Speech

ALICE HAYWARD EDWARDS
A. B., M. Ed.
Office Training, Shorthand

AMY ESTELL WARE
A. B., M. A.
Geography

CAROLINE EDITH PORTER
B. S., M. A.
Literature, Reading, Speech

MILDRED BROWNING STONE
B. S. Ed., A. M.
Mathematics

MIRA WALLACE
B. S. Ed., Ed. M.
Physical Education

LUCY STATEN BELL, B. S.
Librarian

LEON HOWARD ROCKWELL
B. S., A. M.
Education, History

CHARLES FRANCIS WOODS
Music

ELIZABETH ROBERTS
A. B., Ed. M.
English, Business Education

LILLIAN M. HOFF, B. S., M. A.
Special Education

FLORENCE G. PERRY, B. S.
Art

L. GERTRUDE BUNTON
B. S., M. A.
Education

GERTRUDE BURNHAM
A. B., A. M.
English Composition, Literature

EDNA MARY McGLYNN
A. B., A. M., Ph. D.
History, Government

LAWRENCE T. LOWREY, Ph. B.
Physical Education, Logic

MARGARET C. KING
Physical Education

ROGER A. HARDY, B. S., M. B. A.
*Accounting, Business Organization,
Banking*

RICHARD H. ROCKETT
A. B., LL. B. M. Ed.
Latin, French, Commercial Law

MARY M. O'KEEFE
Secretary

ANN KEENAN CLARK
Registrar

Horace Mann Training School

GEORGE FALLOWS MOODY
B. S. Ed., A. M.
Director

Training School Faculty

ESTHER LOUISE SMALL
Supervisor, Grade Seven

HAZEL ELIZABETH ROUNDS
Supervisor, Grade Eight

MARY LILLIAN PERHAM
Supervisor, Grade Five

GLADYS E. MOREHOUSE, B. S. Ed.
Supervisor, Grade Six

DORIS A. CAMBRIDGE
Supervisor, Grade Four

MARY ELIZABETH JAMES
Supervisor, Grade Three

MARY FOSTER WADE, B. S. Ed.
Supervisor, Grade Two

SYBIL INEZ TUCKER
Supervisor, Grade One

ETHEL VERA KNIGHT
Kindergarten

ELEANOR ELIZABETH WALKER
Special Class

GEORGE WILLIAM LITTLE
B. S. Ed.
Practical Arts

VIOLA I. MUNYAN, B. S. ED.
Home Economics

Faculty Directory

SULLIVAN, EDWARD A...16 Pond View Rd., Arlington
BADGER, MARIE................................19 Frederick Street, Framingham
BELL, LUCY ....36 Central Street, Beverly
BUNTON, L. GERTRUDE.....................63 Washington Ave., Cambridge
BURNHAM, GERTRUDE.............................296 Lafayette St., Salem
CRUTTENDEN, FLORENCE.........................18 Raymond Ave., Salem
DONER, CHARLES E.............................43 Scotland Road, Reading
EDWARDS, ALICE H. ....9 Temple Court, Salem
FLANDERS, VERNA B...........................11 Puritan Road, Swampscott
GOLDSMITH, GERTRUDE.....................303 Lafayette Street, Salem
HARDY, ROGER............................35 Harrison Ave., Swampscott
HARRIS, MAUDE L.............................224 Lafayette Street, Salem
HOFF, LILLIAN M............................117 Lafayette Street, Salem
KING, MARGARET C.........................95 Prescott Street, Cambridge
LOWREY, LAWRENCE.......................349 Pleasant Street, Malden
McGLYNN, EDNA M...........................88 McKay Street, Beverly
PERRY, FLORENCE G.......................303 Lafayette Street, Salem
PORTER, CAROLINE E......................254 Lafayette Street, Salem
ROBERTS, ELIZABETH...........................9 Temple Court, Salem
ROCKETT, RICHARD H........................6 Oak Circle, Marblehead
ROCKWELL, LEON H........................300 Lafayette Street, Salem
SPROUL, ALEXANDER H...............132 Asbury Street, South Hamilton
STONE, MILDRED B.........................18 Raymond Avenue, Salem
WALLACE, MIRA...............................27 Linden Street, Salem
WARE, AMY E...............................8 Pierce Street, Marblehead
WHITMAN, WALTER G.........................10 Naples Road, Salem
WOODS, C. FRANCIS.......................28 Elsemere Avenue, Lynn
CLARK, ANN K............................8 Bowden Street, Marblehead
O'KEEFE, MARY M...........................8 Grove Street, Salem

Training School Faculty Directory

MOODY, GEORGE FALLOWS.................3 Sheridan Road, Swampscott
CAMBRIDGE, DORIS A.......................14 Hemenway Road, Salem
JAMES, M. ELIZABETH.........................162 North Street, Salem
KNIGHT, ETHEL VERA......................27 Stephen Street, Lynn
LITTLE, GEORGE W......................96 Oakwood Avenue, Lynn
MOREHOUSE, GLADYS M...................452 Lafayette Street, Salem
MUNYAN, VIOLA I.........................452 Lafayette Street, Salem
PERHAM, MARY.............................266 Lafayette Street, Salem
ROUNDS, HAZEL E.......................452 Lafayette Street, Salem
SMALL, ESTHER L. ....29 Franklin Street, Marblehead
TUCKER, SYBIL I.........................303 Lafayette Street, Salem
WADE, MARY F............................40 Buffum Street, Salem
WALKER, ELEANOR E.......................285 Lafayette Street, Salem

Seniors

J. RICHARD BATH

43 Winnepurkit Avenue, Lynn

Interest—a little
Diffidence—well!
Helpfulness—a lot
Diversity—his creed

Camera Club 1, 2; Dramatic Club 2, 4; Glee Club 1, 2, 3; Commercial Council Treasurer 3; Junior Prom Committee 3; Cooperative Council Auditing Committee 4; Log Reporter 2, Sports Editor 3, Advertising Manager 4; Class Treasurer 4; Executive Board 3.

HENRY PHILIP BAUSH

30 Willow Street, Holyoke

"Butch"
Chair-tilter
Long-fellow
Fugitive from a Russian Revolution

Dramatic Club 1, 2, 3; Treasurer 4; Commercial Council 1, 2, 3, 4; Commercial Banquet Committee 4; Junior Prom Committee; Senior Reception Committee; Commercial Representative; Basketball 2, 3.

YVONNE EMILIENNE BERNARDIN

635 HAVERHILL STREET, LAWRENCE

Stately
Joan of Arc
Tres Jolie
Tickets—tickets—tickets

Glee Club 1; International Relations Club 2; Book Club 3. Vice-president 4; Publicity Committee; *Log* Staff Secretary; *Clipper* Assistant Editor; Field Hockey 1, 2, honor team 3; coach 4; Basketball 1, coach 3, 4; Volleyball 1; Newcomb 2; Bowling 2; Tennis 2, 3; Cooperative Council Representative 2; President's List 2, 4; Daisy Chain 3.

ARTHUR N. BOUDREAU

6 ARTHUR AVENUE, LOWELL

"Rhapsody in Blue"
Esquire
Educational traveler
A willing helper

Camera Club 3; International Relations Club 4; Pitman Debating Society 4; Senior Reception Orchestra Committee 4; *Clipper* Advertising Manager 4; Council Representative 3, 4; Baccalaureate Usher 2, 3; President's List 2, 3, 4.

HERBERT BRENNER

43 Prospect Street, Lynn

Ace in sports
Ace in studies
Ace in the hearts
Of the Mademoiselles

Dramatic Club 4; MAA Executive Board 2, 3, Secretary 4; Cooperative Council Committee; Financial Committee 4; Basketball 1, 4, Captain 2, 3, New England Conference Basketball Team 1, 2, 3; Baseball 1, 2, 3, Captain 4; Softball 4; Prseident's List 2, 3; Graduation Usher 3; Class Day Usher 3; New England Teacher Preparation Conference Delegate 2; Baccalaureate Usher 2.

IRENE MARY CARRAHER

72 Nesmith Street, Lawrence

Recitation
Determination
Basketball-itation
Midge

Dramatic Club 1, 2, 3, 4; Commercial Council 2; Hockey 1, 2, Honor Team 3, 4; Basketball 1, 2, 3, 4; Newcomb 1, 2, 3; Volleyball 1, 2, 3; Baseball 1, 2; Bowling 1, 2; President's List 4.

ALBERT CONLON

4A Larch Road, Lynn

Punster
Dictator of Pinehill
"Mr. and Mrs."
Frat Wit

Dramatic Club 1, 2, 3, 4; Glee Club 1, 2, 4; Secretary-Treasurer 3; Social Committee; Junior Prom Decorating Committee 3; Outing Committee 4; Senior Reception Committee 4; MAA President 4; Commercial Council 1, 3; Baseball 1.

PENELOPE HALLAS DeCOULOS

29 Oak Street, Peabody

Busy fingers
Shiny Penny
Cheery chatter
Is this our freshman?

Craft Club 2; Commercial Council 1, 2, 3, 4; Camera Club 3, 4; Tri Mu 1, 2; *Clipper*, Typist 1, Secretary 4; *Log* Reporter 3, 4; Volleyball 1, 3; Tennis 1; Soccer 1, 2, 3; Basketball 1; Bowling 1, 2; Field Hockey 2, 3; Modern Dance 1; Fieldball 1, 2, 3; Newcomb 1, 2; Commercial Senior Class Secretary 4.

JOHN U. DONAHUE

15 HAZEL STREET, HAVERHILL

Self-assured
Book of knowledge
Perpetual debater
S. T. C. taxi

Mathematics Club 2; Debating Club 2, President 3, Advisory Board 4; International Relations Club 4; *Clipper* Advertising Manager 4; *Log* Reporter 3, 4; Junior Varsity Basketball 2, 3, 4.

JOHN DONEGAN

16 STEPHEN STREET, LYNN

A Doner-gan
Still waters
Hay-man of affairs
Don Juan

Dramatic Club 4; Glee Club 1, 2, 3, 4; Auditing Committee 2; MAA Executive Board 4; Baseball 1, 2, 4; Softball 4.

FLORENCE MURIEL EISENBERG

8 BAKER ROAD, NAHANT

A touch of spice
A dash of color
Rhythmic grace
Vogue

Girl's Glee Club 1, 2; Commercial Council; Travel Club 3; Camera Club 4; Junior Prom Committee 3; Basketball 1, 2, 4; Golf 3; Badminton 2, 4; Tennis 1, 2; Bowling 2, 4; Volleyball 2; Newcomb 1; Laurel Chain 3.

DOROTHY L. FIELD

29 TROY STREET, LOWELL

8:19 wave
Quiet poise
My dear lady
Dainty Dot

Dramatic Club 3, 4; Commercial Council 1, 2, 3, 4; Newcomb 1; Commercial Council Representative 2.

34

SAMUEL FINKLE

25 Crosby Street, Lynn

Super-salesman
What 'ta 'tory?
Debonair
"Ball-player"

Dramatic Club 1, 2, 3, 4; Camera Club 1, 2; Glee Club 1, 2, 3, 4; MAA Executive Board 4; *Compass* Committee 4; Junior Prom Orchestra Committee Chairman 3; Class Finance Committee 1; *Clipper* Business Manager 4; Basketball 1, 2, 3, Captain 4; Baseball 1, 2; Junior Varsity Basketball Coach 3, 4; College Choir 3, 4.

FRANCIS JOHN GILMORE

119 Tremont Street, Peabody

Dapper
"Little Man Who Wasn't There"
Often pursued—never conquered
Manana

Glee Club 1, 3, Treasurer 2; Dramatic Club 4; Cooperative Council Finance Committee 4; MAA Executive Board 1, Secretary 2, President 3; Baseball 1, 2, 3, 4; Golf 2, 3; Baccalaureate Usher; Class Day Usher.

GERTRUDE MAY GURIN

160 Chestnut Street, Cambridge

A Dale Carnegie
First Nighter
Intrepid
"So what?"

Glee Club 1; Craft Club 2; Travel Club 3, Co-chairman 4; Commercial Council 1, 2, 3, 4; Fieldball 1, 2; Basketball 1, 2, Coach 3, 4; Bowling 1, 2, 3; Newcomb 1, 2, 3; Volleyball 1, 2, Coach 3; Badminton 2, 3; Tenikoit 2, 3; Field Hockey Honor Team 1, 2, 3, 4; Soccer 3, Honor Team and Coach 4; Tennis 1.

MARY LOUISE HARTNETT

46 WALTER STREET, SALEM

Harris tweeds
Salem's Bernhardt
Brightly "Burns" a flame
Loquacious

Tri Mu 1; Pitman Debating Society 1, 2,
Secretary 3, 4; Dramatic Club 3, 4; Commercial Council 1, 2, 3, 4; Junior Prom Committee 3; Social Committee 2, 3; WAA
Head of Bowling 2, Secretary 3; *Log* Cir-
culation Manager 3, Business Manager 4;
Clipper Business Manager 4; Hockey 4.
Honor Team 1, 2, 3; Newcomb 2, 3; Volleyball 1, 2, 3, 4; Basketball 1, 2, 3, 4; Bowling
1, 2, 3; Tennis 1; Baseball 1; Badminton 2,
3, 4; Golf 3; Soccer 3; President's List 2, 3;
Baccalaureate Usher 2; Laurel Chain 3;
Commercial Council Representative; Saluta-
torian 4.

BEATRICE ARLENE HULBERT

58 BUFFUM STREET, SALEM

Lovely to look at
Delightful to know
Kind and considerate
Photographer's model

Tri Mu 1, 2, 4; Commercial Council Representative 3, 4; Commercial Council President 4; Basketball 1, 2; Hockey 1, 4.
Honor Team 2; Volleyball 2, 3; Bowling
1, 2.

ANGIE ANTHEA JOHNSON

10 HANNATT STREET, IPSWICH

Active in sports
Tiny in stature
Great in spirit
Steadfast in action

Commercial Council 1, 2, 3, 4; Craft Club Secretary-Treasurer 2; Camera Club 3, Program Committee 4; *Log* Reporter 4; *Clipper* Associate Editor 4; Fieldball 2; Soccer 3, Honor Team 4; Newcomb 1, 2, 3; Volleyball 1; Basketball 1, 2, 3; Bowling 1, 2, 3; Baseball 1; Modern Dance 3; Golf 3; Hockey Honor Team 1, 2, 3, 4; Tennis 1; Tenikoit 1, 2; Badminton 3; Girl Scouts 4.

MAY MILDRED KAPLAN

71 CHATHAM ROAD, EVERETT

Managerial
Traveler's helper
"In my town——"
Destination determined

Glee Club 1; Craft Club 2; Travel Club 3, 4; Commercial Council 1, 2, 3, 4; Basketball 1, 2, 4. Captain 3; Hockey 1, 2, 3; Fieldball 1, 2, 3; Volleyball 1, 2, 3, 4; Badminton 1, 2, 3; Tenikoit 1, 2, 3; Baseball 1, 2, 3; Soccer 1, 2, 3, 4; Newcomb 1, 2, 3; Bowling 1, 2, 3; Hiking 1, 2, 3, 4.

MARY R. KELTY

69 So. Loring Street, Lowell

Rustle of taffeta
Two bright blue eyes
Not a hair out of place
Miss Secretary

Glee Club 1, 2; Commercial Council 1, 2, 3, 4; Book Club 4; Social Committee 1; Newcomb 1; Basketball 2; Council Representative 2; President's List 3.

JOSEPHINE T. KOCHANSKA

57 Seventh Street, Cambridge

For God and country
Black-eyed Susan
Evening glitter
True blue

Camera Club 3; Dramatic Club 4; Commercial Council 1, 2, 3, 4; Senior Reception Decoration Committee 4; Newcomb 1; Field Hockey 4.

MANTINA LEFTHES

11 Ward Street, Salem

Sh-h-h!!
Burnished copper
Charm in abundance
Out-door girl

Tri mu 1, 2, 3, 4; Travel Club 3, Co-chairman 4; Commercial Council 1, 2, 3, 4; Senior Reception Committee 4; *Clipper* Typist 1; Volleyball 1, 2, 3; Basketball 4, Honor Team 1, 2, 3; Baseball 1; Fieldball 2; Newcomb 2, 3; Bowling 2, 3; Hockey 1, 4.

ELEANOR NATALIE LOITMAN

22 Jefferson Avenue, Chelsea

Effervescent vivacity
Laughter and music
Staccato in French heels
Youthfully yours

Dramatic Club 1, 2; Debating Club 4; Senior Reception Ticket Committee 4; Hockey Honor Team 1, 2; Badminton 2, 3, 4; Volleyball 2, 3, 4; Soccer 3; Fieldball 1, 2; Basketball 1, 2, 3, 4; Bowling 1, 2, 3, 4; Baseball 1, 2, 3; Newcomb 1, 2; Daisy Chain 3.

JAMES THOMAS McKINLAY

120 Lawton Avenue, Lynn

Smoothie
Head of softball
Bing's understudy
Freshmen's fancy

Glee Club 1, 2, 3, 4; Dramatic Club 4; Council Auditing Committee Chairman 4; Junior Prom Invitation and Decoration Committees 3; Senior Reception Committee 4; MAA Treasurer 2, Vice President 4; Commercial Council Representative 1; Basketball 1, 2, 3, 4; Baccaulaureate Usher 2.

KATHLEEN JANE MEDEIROS

3 Winthrop Place, Provincetown

Friendly
Star boarder
Always prepared
Cape-Codder

Travel Club 4; Commercial Council 1, 2, 3, 4; Typing Award 1.

MARY MOONEY

10 Violet Street, Lynn

Reserved
Busy
Capable
Little lady

Dramatic Club 2; Book Club 4; Archery 3;
Modern Dance 2; Typing Award 1.

ANNA KARIN NELSON

101 West Quincy Street, West Somerville

Swede as sugar
Camellia complexion
4:15 rush
winsome wench

Dramatic Club 3, 4; Commercial Council 1,
2, 3, 4; Newcomb 1.

ALMA RUTH NORTON

33 McKinley Avenue, Lowell

Smiling
"Angel"
Unperturbed calm
Sweet words

Dramatic Club 3, 4; Commercial Club 1, 2, 3, 4; Newcomb 1.

HILDA PEARLMUTTER

247 Campbell Avenue, Revere

Quizzical
Nonchalant
I. Q.-nacious
Expert forgettory

Glee Club 1, 2; Dramatic Club 3; Camera Club 4; Commercial Club 1, 2, 3, 4; Basketball 1, 2, 4; Fieldball 1, 2; Archery 2, 3; Tennis 1, 2; Bowling 3; Hockey 3

MURIEL FRANCES POIRIER

36 Forest Street, Peabody

Breath of femininity
Mademoiselle
Background for gracious living
Gentle mannered

Tri Mu 2, 3, 4; Commercial Club 1, 2, 3, 4; Travel Club 3, 4; *Clipper* Secretary 4; Basketball 2, 3, 4; Field Hockey 4; Newcomb 2, 3, 4; Volleyball 2, 3, 4; Bowling 2, 3, 4; Official, Play Day 3.

ETTA LOUISE QUEENAN

6 Olive Street, Lowell

Giggles galore
Etta-quette
Coquetta
"Have you heard this one?"

Dramatic Club 3, 4; Girl Scouts; Newcomb 1, 2.

JANE REED

35 Walter Street, Salem

Ever bustling
Ever hustling
Ever dubious
Ever studious

Tri Mu 1, 2, 4; Travel Club 3, 4; Craft Club 2; Commercial Council 1, 2, 3, 4; Basketball 2, 3; Newcomb 1, 2; Baseball 1; Volleyball 1, 2, 3; Hockey 2, 3; Fieldball 1, 2; Soccer 3; Bowling 2, 3; Tennis 1; Tenikoit 1, 2; Girl Scouts 3 ,4; President's List 3, 4; Laurel Chain 3.

M. LORRAINE RODERICK

51 Walnut Avenue, Revere

A twinkle in her eye
A laughing lilt to her voice
A charm all her own
A lot of Forte-tude

Glee Club 1; International Relations Club 2; Travel Club 3; Dramatic Club 4; Senior Reception Ticket Committee 4; *Log* Reporter 1, 2; Fieldball 1; Hockey 2, 4, Honor Team 3; Baseball 1, 2; Volleyball 1, 2, 3, 4; Basketball 1, 2, 3, 4; Bowling 2, 3, 4; Tennis 1; Badminton 2, 3; Golf 3, 4; Newcomb 1, 2; Tenikoit 2, 3; Soccer Honor Team 3; Laurel Chain 3; Baccalaureate Usher 2; President's List 4.

AMELIA BLANCHE ROMBULT

283 Main Street, Lynnfield Center

Melody from the sky
Eager to help
Amelia-bility
Polish correspondence

Glee Club 1, 2, 4; Travel Club Secretary 3; Girl Scouts 3, 4; Tri Mu 4; Commercial Council 1, 2, 3, 4; WAA Banquet Program Chairman 3; Basketball 1, Coach 2, 3, 4; Volleyball 1, Coach 2, 3, 4; Newcomb 1, 2, 3, 4; Field Hockey 4; Archery 1, 2; Tenikoit 1, 2, 3; Bowling 2, 3, 4; Golf 3; Badminton 2, 3, 4; Baseball 1, 2; Tennis 1, 2.

AARON ROWSEMITT

35 Prospect Street, Lynn

Handy Andy
Subtle gentleman
A man of affairs
"I'll do it."

Pitman Debating Society 1, 3, Manager 2, Executive Board 4; Camera Club 4; Glee Club 1, 2, 3, 4; *Compass* Committee Chairman 3; Council Publicity Committee 3, 4; *Log* Reporter 1, News Editor 2, Associate Editor 3, Makeup Editor 4; Columbia Press Association Conference Delegate 3; Second Hand Bookstore Chairman 4.

ALICE VERONICA SAWYER

281 South Broadway, Lawrence

Sports a-plenty
Careful driver
Cheery smile
Carefree manner

WAA Secretary 4; Dramatic Club 2, 3; Commercial Club 1, 2, 3, 4; Fieldball 2, 3; Field hockey 2, 4; Soccer 2; Newcomb 2, 3; Volleyball 1, 2, 3; Bowling 2, 3, 4; Badminton 2, 4; Baseball 1, 2; Tennis 1; Tenikoit 2; Basketball 1, Honor Team 2, Coach 3, 4; Girl Scouts 3, 4.

LOUISE ELAINE SIDERI

258A Chatham Street, Lynn

A Schiaparelli model
Unjoltable calm
Sophistication
Real study

Dramatic Club 2; Book Club 4; Junior Prom Ticket Committee 3; Archery 3; Modern Dance 2; Typing Award 1.

47

JOSEPH A. SULLIVAN

117 WATERHILL STREET, LYNN

A witty tongue
Earnest endeavor
Rescue the heroine or raise Keane
Leader in all

Dramatic Club 2, 3, 4; Debating Club 1, 2, 3, 4; Men's Glee Club; Junior Prom Committee 3; Cooperative Council President 4, Vice President 3; Amendment Committee 3; Bookstore Committee 3; Class President; *Log* Sports Editor 2; Managing Editor 3; Basketball 1, 2, 3, 4; Baseball 1, 2, 3; President's List 2, 4; New York Conference 2; New England Teachers Preparation Association Conference Delegate 3, 4.

BARBARA ALLEN SWAN

35 ST. JOHN STREET, JAMAICA PLAIN

Magazine cover smile
Magnetic personality
Mite but mighty clever
"Miss Mischief"

Camera Club 3; Dramatic Club 4; Commercial Council 1, 2, 3, 4; *Clipper* Literary Editor; Hockey 1, Honor Team 3; Basketball 1, 4; President's List 3, 4.

KATHRYN SWEENEY

25 TREMONT STREET, PEABODY

Keen mind, kind heart
Comely? We'll say!
Carefree, yet queenly
That's our Kay

Glee Club 1; Travel Club 2; International
Relations Club 3; Dramatic Club 4; Audit-
ing Committee 2; Assembly Committee 3, 4;
Junior Prom Ticket Committee Chairman 3;
Council Dance Committee 2, 3; WAA Nom-
inating Committee 4, Head of Newcomb 2,
Head of Hockey 3; Volleyball 1, 2, 3, 4;
Basketball 1, 2, 3, 4; Newcomb 1, 2; Hockey
1, 2, 3, 4; Baseball 1, 2; Bowling 1, 2, 3, 4;
Badminton 2, 3, 4; Tenikoit 2, 3, 4; Field-
ball 1; Tennis 1; Golf 3, 4; Cooperative
Council Representative 1; Daisy Chain 3;
Baccalaureate Usher 2; Senior Reception
Usher 3; President's List 2, 3, 4; New York
Convention 3.

LLOYD EVERETT TRIPP

490 CHICOPEE STREET, WILLIMANSETT

Impeccable attire
Gallant
An eye for detail
"Emily Post says . . ."

Dramatic Club 1, 2, 3, 4; Camera Club 4;
Commercial Club 1, 2, 3, 4; Glee Club 1, 2,
3, 4; Junior Prom Committee 3; Senior
Reception Committee 4; *Clipper* Secretary 4.

FRANCES MARY BUCKLEY

15 Lyman Street, Beverly

She went to the ant
Approved his ways
Applied them to
Buckley Project 999

Glee Club 1, 2; Association for Childhood Education 1; Camera Club 3, 4. Junior Prom Decoration Committee 3; Cooperative Council Handbook Committee Chairman 3; Clipper Dance Publicity Committee 4; *Log* Headline Writer and Reporter 2, 3; News Editor 4; Baseball 2; Bowling 2; Basketball 1, 2, 3; Fieldball 1, 2; Field Hockey 2; Newcomb 1, 2; Modern Dance 2; Volleyball 1, 2, 3.

FRANCIS P. DRABINOWICZ

17 Daniels Street, Salem

The polka
Happy-go-lucky
Opinions unlimited
Enthusiasm likewise

Camera Club 1, 2, 3; International Relations Club 4; Basketball 3; Track 3.

WILLIAM FINE

1405 Blue Hill Avenue, Mattapan

Serious
And so naif
A friendly grin
A baffled frown

Camera Club 2, 3, 4; Baseball 1, 2, 3, 4; Basketball 4; Junior Varsity 1, 2, 3; Football 1, 2; Graduation Usher 3.

JOSEPH C. FORTE

39 Medford Street, Medford

Highly-concentrated energy
A bit of temperament
Hustle-bustle

John Burroughs Club 1, Executive Board 2, Publicity Director 3, President 4; Social Committee 2, 3, 4; Junior Prom Orchestra Committee 3; *Clipper* Dance Ticket Committee 4; Senior Reception Orchestra Committee 4; M. A. A. Executive Board 1, 2, 3, 4; Baseball 1, 2, 3, Captain 4; Basketball Junior Varsity 1, Varsity 2, 3, 4; Track 2; Class Day Usher 3; Graduation Usher 3; Baccalaureate Usher 2.

SHIRLEY FREDMAN

313 Shirley Street, Winthrop

Echoes of Beethoven
Dressmaker's delight
Book lover
Sophisticate

Craft Club 2; Book Club 3, Treasurer 4; *Log* reporter 2, 3; Newcomb 2, 3; Tennis 1, 2; Ping Pong 1, 2, 3, 4; Bowling 2; Tenikoit 2.

ROSELLA M. GALLAGHER

13 Aerial Street, Arlington

Cherub—
With a tilted halo
Dimples
And a merry laugh

Pitman Debating Society 1, 2, 3, 4; Glee Club 1; Camera Club 2; International Relations Club Librarian 4; Class Finance Committee 1; Junior Prom Decoration Committee 3; *Clipper* Dance Decoration Committee 4; Class Treasurer 1, W. A. A. Head of Tennis 3; *Clipper* Associate Editor 4; Fieldball 1, 2; Field Hockey 1, 3, Honor Team 2; Basketball 1, 2, 3; Baseball 1, 2; Bowling 1, 2; Archery 1; Volleyball 1, 2, 3; Badminton 1, 2, 3, 4; Tennis 1, 2; Tenikoit 1, 2, 3; President's List 3, 4; Council Representative 4; New England Teacher Training Conference 1.

ELLSWORTH N. GETCHELL

3 Vincent Street, Saugus

Genial
Unfailing good nature
Right-hand man
The proverbial open book

Camera Club Treasurer 1, Vice President 2,
3, Co-President 4; Junior Prom Decoration
Committee 3; *Clipper* Dance Decoration
Committee 4; Outing Committee 4; *Clipper*
Photography Editor 4; Junior Varsity Bas-
ketball 2, 4; Track 2; Graduation Usher 3;
Class Day Usher 3; Baccalaureate Usher 2;
President's List 4.

HOPE HILTON

1 Myrtle Square, Gloucester

Incorrigible punster
Unsquelchable inquisitor
Saint Cecelia of S. T. C.
"Onward, Christian Soldiers"

Glee Club Accompanist 1, 2, 3, 4; Junior
Prom Decoration Committee 3; Fieldball
Honor Team 1, 2; Modern Dance 2; Soccer
3, Honor Team 4; Basketball 1, 2, 3, 4;
Hockey 2, 3, 4; Newcomb 1, 2; Volleyball 1;
Archery 1.

RUTH MARGARET KEANE

26 Franklin Street, Peabody

Radiant
Vivacious
Cameo profile
Zest for living

Dramatic Club 1; Glee Club 2, 3, 4; Tri Mu 2, 3, 4; Junior Prom Co-Chairman Decoration Committee 3; Senior Reception Refreshment Committee 4; Outing Committee Chairman 4; Class Executive Board 2, 3; W. A. A. Harvard Captain 2, Manager of Sports 3, President 4; Fieldball 1, 2; Field Hockey 1, 2, 3, 4; Basketball 1, 2, 3, 4; Newcomb 1, 2; Volleyball 1, 2, 3, 4; Baseball 1; Bowling 1; Badminton 1, 2, 3, 4; Archery 1, 2; Tenikoit 1, 2, 3; Tennis 1, 2; "Harmony Hall" 2, "Enchanted Isle" 3; College Choir 2, 3, 4; President's List 2, 4; Baccalaureate Exercises 2, 3; Daisy Chain 3; W. A. A. Conference—North Adams 3, Fitchburg 4; New England Teachers College Conference 4; Bridgewater-Salem Sports Day Official 3; Council Representative 1, 2, 3.

MARJORIE KINCAID

86 Bromfield Road, Somerville

Sunny smile
A cure for the blues
Opera booster
Globe-trotter

Craft Club 2; Camera Club 2, 3, Assistant Business Manager 4; Girl Scout Treasurer 3.

ELEANOR SHIRLEY KNOWLES

INDIAN RIDGE, IPSWICH

A true New Englander
Uncompromising opinions
Emphatically expressed—
Suddenly an impish grin

John Burroughs Club 1; Craft Club Vice
President 2; Book Club 3; *Log* Reporter 1,
2, 3; Newcomb 1, 2; Volleyball 1, 2; Head
of Girl Scout Troop 3, 4; Assistant Chapel
Pianist 3, 4; President's List 2, 3, 4.

MARY A. KOROSKYS

3 ABBOTT STREET, NORTH ANDOVER

Cassandra complex
Ingenuous
The immortalizer of
Little Rose Elf

Dramatic Club 1; Craft Club 2; Camera
Club 3, 4; Field Hockey 1, 4, Honor Team
2, 3; Basketball 1, 2; Soccer 1, 2, 3; Archery
1, 2.

RUTH LaPORTE

WINTER ISLAND, SALEM

Stately
Lovely
Witty—but
"I don't get it!"

Glee Club 1, 3, 4, Librarian 2; Tri Mu 1, 4, Secretary 2, President 3; General Welfare Committee 2, 3, Chairman 4; Senior Reception General Chairman 4; *Clipper* Dance Orchestra Committee 4; Class Vice President 4; W. A. A. Head of Hiking 2, Recording Secretary 3, Treasurer 4; Field Hockey 1; Fieldball 2; Newcomb 1, 2; Volleyball 1, 2; Basketball 1, 2, 3, 4; Bowling 2; College Choir 2, 3, 4; Daisy Chain Marshal 3.

RUTH LEVIN

25 CROSBY STREET, LYNN

A sense of humor
Irons in the fire
Goddess of finance
Metropolitan outlook

International Relations Club 1, 2, 4, Secretary 3; Handbook Committee 3; General Welfare Committee 3; Junior Prom Publicity Committee 3; *Clipper* Dance Publicity Committee 4; Custodian of Banking Fund 1, 2, 3, 4; Class Treasurer 2; W. A. A. Head of Basketball 3; *Log* Reporter 1, 2, Sports Editor 3; Cooperative Council Vice President 4; Fieldball 2; Field Hockey 2, 4; Basketball Honor Team 2, 3, 4; Volleyball 1, 2; Newcomb 1, 2; Baseball 1; Bowling 2; New York Conference 3; Laurel Chain 3; Bridgewater-Salem Basketball Play Day Chairman 3; President's List 3; New England Teacher Training Conference 3, 4.

LOUISE M. MOULTON

91 UNION STREET, SOUTH HAMILTON

Philosophical
Perspicacious
Caustic quips
And all the answers

Glee Club 1, 2, Treasurer 4; *Clipper* Dance General Chairman 4; *Clipper* Editor-in-Chief 4; President's List 2, 3, 4; College Choir 2; Valedictorian 4.

RENA C. PEDRONI

16 QUARRY STREET, GLOUCESTER

Sweet and lovely
Moonlight
Spring Song
Invitation to the dance

Glee Club 1, 2, Secretary 3, Vice President 4; Cooperative Council Finance Committee 3, Chairman 4; Junior Prom Co-Chairman Decoration Committee 3; Class Treasurer 3; W. A. A. Junior High Representative 3, Head of Basketball 4; *Log* Reporter 1, 2, 3; Basketball 1, 2, 3, 4; Hockey Honor Team 2, 4; Volleyball 1, 2, 3; Newcomb 1, 2; Bowling 1, 2, 3, 4; Baseball 1; Fieldball 2; Daisy Chain 3; College Choir 2, 3, 4.

RUTH LUCILLE PRESCOTT

POND STREET, GEORGETOWN

Incomparable serenity
A little cottage
Robins and roses
"O Promise Me"

Girls' Glee Club 2, 3, President 4; Assembly Committee 2, 4, Chairman 3; Bowling 1; Volleyball 1, 2; Basketball 1, 2; Fieldball 1. 2; Newcomb 2; Field Hockey 2; "Enchanted Isle" 3; President's List 2, 3; College Choir 2, 3, 4; Girl Scout Troop Scribe 3; Daisy Chain 3.

SYLVIA PRESCOTT

103 WILLOW STREET, MALDEN

Poise
Warm generosity
Letter mania
Poetry cutter-outer

Dramatic Club 1, 2, Secretary 3, Vice President 4; Junior Prom Decoration Committee 3; W. A. A. Harvard Captain 3, Head of Dancing 4; *Log* Reporter 1, 2, 3; Fieldball 1, 2; Field Hockey 1, 2, 3, 4; Basketball 1, 2, 3; Bowling 1; Newcomb 1, 2; Volleyball 1, 2, 3; Baseball 1; Modern Dance 2, 3, 4; Coach of *The Barretts* 4.

OLGA LAURETTE SAPP

368 SOUTH UNION STREET, LAWRENCE

Twinkling eyes
Dancing feet
Ready laughter
And a determined chin

Book Club 3; International Relations Club Social Committee Chairman 4; Junior Prom Decoration Committee; Basketball 1, 2, 3; Baseball 1, 2; Hockey 1, Honor Team 2, 3, 4; Bowling 1, 2, 3; Soccer 2, 3; Volleyball 2, 3.

CLARA ELIZABETH SCHIORRING

12 BALLARD STREET, SAUGUS

A peach of a girl
With a love of dancing
Dark curls
A tilt of the head

Dramatic Club 1; Glee Club 2, 3, 4; Junior Prom Program Committee 3; Volleyball 1; Basketball 2, 3, 4; Hockey 3, Honor Team 2; Tenikoit 2, 3; Bowling 1; Badminton 3; Laurel Chain 3.

ALFONSO SUDENTAS

ROGERS AVENUE, DEDHAM

Mercurial speed
Sesquipedalian words
Magnanimous nature
"He's a good kid"

Mathematics Club 1; Camera Club 2, Treasurer 3; International Relations Club 4; *Log* Photographer 2, 3, 4; Graduation Usher 3.

MARGARET JEAN SUTHERLAND

171 HOLTEN STREET, DANVERS

Poetic
Idealistic
Fragile
Hi, Demosthenes!

International Relations Club 2, Treasurer 3, President 4; *Clipper* Dance Invitation Committee 4; *Clipper* Literary Editor 4; Laurel Chain 3; Declamation Contest Second Prize 1, First Prize 2.

MADELINE TOBIN

7 MELVILLE PLACE, LYNN

Jovial companionship
Westward Ho!
Stage and home
"Well, my Dad says—"

Dramatic Club 1; Craft Club 2; Book Club Vice President 3, President 4; Fieldball 1, 2, 3; Hockey 1, 2, 3; Basketball 2, 3; Bowling 2, 3; Badminton 3; Girl Scout Patrol Leader 2.

BERTHA L. WAHL

MAIN STREET, TOPSFIELD

A characteristic stride
Peanuts and hockey
A good sport
And good at sports

International Relations Club Social Committee Co-chairman 4; Hockey 1, Honor Team 2, 3; Baseball 1; Basketball 1, 2, 3, 4; Soccer 1, 2; Bowling 1, 2; Newcomb 1, 2, 3; Volleyball 1, 2, 3.

LETITIA MARIE WATSON

North Street, Georgetown

Independent
Outspoken
Indomitable
Rugged individualist

Glee Club 2; Book Club Treasurer 3; *Clipper* Dance Invitation Committee 4; Soccer 1, 2; Newcomb 1, 2; Basketball 1, 2, 3; Volleyball 1, 2; Field Hockey 1, 2, Honor Team 3; Laurel Chain.

SOPHIE N. ZETES

185 Franklin Street, Lynn

Athletic
Reliable
Industrious
Swing enthusiastic

Glee Club 1, 2, 3, Secretary 4; Hockey 4, Honor Team 2, 3; Basketball 1, 2, 3, Honor Team 4; Volleyball 1, 2, 3, 4; Bowling 1, 2; Baseball 1; Fieldball 1; Newcomb 1, 2; Badminton 2, 3; Tenikoit 1, 2, 3; President's List 3, 4.

GEORGE C. ZOULIAS

224 Auburn Street, Manchester,
New Hampshire

Exuberant
Aggressive
Man about town
New Hampshire, rah!

John Burroughs Club 4; Senior Reception Committee 4; Basketball 4; Graduate of Keene Normal School, 1935.

HELEN R. BALDWIN

63 BAKER ROAD, EVERETT

Efficient
Determined
Placidly witty
Conqueror of quizzes

Association for Childhood Education 2, 3, 4; Craft Club 1, 2; Travel Club 4; Finance Committee 2; Social Committee Associate Member 4; *Clipper* Dance Decoration Committee 4, Art Staff 4; Newcomb 4; President's List 2, 3, 4, Commencement Speaker 4.

MELBA BALTZER

81 LAIGHTON STREET, LYNN

Intellectual
Industrious
The practical type
"Got your Economics done?"

Association for Childhood Education 3, 4; Travel Club 4.

NECHAMA BENKOWITZ

136 Shawmut Street, Chelsea

Reserved
Individual
Quiet humor
An ever-acquiring mind

John Burroughs Club 1, 2; Association for Childhood Education 4; Hockey 1; Basketball 1; Volleyball 2; Modern Dancing 2.

RUTH MADELEINE BROOKS

17 Cedar Street, Somerville

Demure
Unassuming
A subdued air
Just call her "Butch."

Association for Childhood Education 4; Craft Club 4; *Clipper* Dance Decoration Committee 4; *Clipper* Art Staff 4.

HARRIET CAMERON

11 Endicott Street, Saugus

Red gold
Laughingly gay
Breath of Spring
Deep in a dream

Glee Club 1, 2; Association for Childhood Education 4; Junior Prom Program Committee 3; Fieldball 1; Archery 1; Hiking 2; Modern Dance 2; Tenikoit 3.

RITA MARIE COTTER

134 Vernal Street, Everett

Cordiality
Quiet accomplishment
Peaches and cream
Goldilocks with a haircut

Association for Childhood Education 1, 2, 3, 4; Craft Club 2; Sketch Club 2; Travel Club 4; Senior Reception Decoration Committee 4; Clipper Dance Ticket Committee 4; Clipper Associate Editor 4; Archery 1; Baseball 1; Fieldball 1, 2; Hockey 1, 2; Hiking 1, 2; Newcomb 2; President's List 3.

RUTH ELIZABETH CRONIN

34 Pleasant Street, Wakefield

Carefree
Debonair
Coppery crown
Merry madcap

Glee Club 1, 4; Association for Childhood Education 3, 4; Junior Prom Refreshment Committee 3; Volleyball 1; Archery 1; Hockey 4.

HELEN MARIE ENOS

358 Lowell Street, Somerville

Sprightly and petite
Joyous laughter
Moonlight and roses
An artist's touch

Junior Prom Program Committee Chairman 3; *Clipper* Dance Decoration Committee 4; *Clipper* Art Staff 4; Senior Reception Decoration Committee 4; Cooperative Council Representative 4; Newcomb 1.

HARRIETT B. ESTY

PARK STREET, NORTH READING

Congenial
Enthusiastic
Outdoor girl
Every minute accounted for

Tri Mu 3; Craft Club 4; Association for Childhood Education 1, 3, 4; *Clipper* Dance Refreshment Committee 4; Basketball 1, 2, 3, 4; Hockey 1; Baseball 1; Daisy Chain 3.

BERTHA ALICE EVANS

14 WALDEN AVENUE, SAUGUS

Moderate
Sympathetic
Assistance galore
Geog. enthusiast

Glee Club 1, 4; Mathematics Club 2; Camera Club 3; Association for Childhood Education 3, 4; Tennis 1, 2; Basketball 1, 2; Newcomb 1, 2; Badminton 1, 2.

ANGELINA IANDOLI

22 Norwood Avenue, Somerville

Wistful
Appealing
Persistency plus
Accent on youth

Travel Club 4; John Burroughs Club 1, 2, Secretary 3; Association for Childhood Education 4; Junior Prom Program Committee 3; *Clipper* Dance Ticket Committee 4; Newcomb 1; Basketball 2.

HELEN MARTHA KELLY

20 Porter Street, Malden

Affable
Diligent
A helping hand
The 4:13 or die

Association for Childhood Education 3, 4; Camera Club 3; Glee Club 4; Hockey 1; Tenikoit 1; Volleyball 1; Newcomb 1; Operetta 3.

MARION LOUISE GRAVES

PELHAM ROAD, AMHERST

A jaunty air
Bit o' merrie England
Individualistic
Marionette

Association for Childhood Education 2; Tri Mu 3, 4; Art Club 4; Social Committee 2, 3; *Clipper* Dance Refreshment Committee 4; Tennis 2, 3; Basketball 3; Daisy Chain 3.

AGNES HAYES

35 SYDNEY STREET, SOMERVILLE

Jolly
Winsome
Plenty of zip
And right now she's got a date

Glee Club 4; Association for Childhood Education 4; Junior Prom Refreshment Committee 3; Laurel Chain 3.

DOROTHY B. LARRABEE

18 Sherman Street, Beverly

Artistic
Dependable
Like a good book
A perfect companion

Camera Club 1, 2, Secretary 3; Association for Childhood Education 1, 4; Travel Club 4; Cooperative Council Social Committee 2, 4, Chairman 3; *Clipper* Dance Decoration Committee Chairman 4, *Clipper* Editor 4; Senior Reception , Decoration Committee Chairman 4; Newcomb 1; Basketball 3; Modern Dancing 3; Daisy Chain 3; Cooperative Council Representative 1, 2.

FRANCES MARY LeBLANC

32 New Park Street, Lynn

Zestful
Persuasive
Distinctive giggle
Prone to moments musicale

Glee Club 1, 3, 4; Mathematics Club 2; Association for Childhood Education 1, 2, 3, 4.

BESSIE MANOLAKIS

15 Abington Avenue, Peabody

A natural artist
Tall
Stately
Truly a Greek goddess

Travel Club 4; Association for Childhood Education 4; Junior Prom Decoration Committee 3; Senior Reception Decoration Committee 4; Clipper Dance Decoration Committee 4; Newcomb 1; Volleyball 1; Basketball 1, 2; Hiking 1, 2.

BARBARA E. MILLER

28 Evans Road, Marblehead

Spontaneous
Endeavoring
Bursts of originality
A little boy asking questions

Association for Childhood Education 4; Glee Club 2; Craft Club President 4; WAA Nominating Board 4; Outing Committee 4; Clipper Dance Publicity Committee 4; Clipper Associate Editor 4; Fieldball 2; Newcomb 2; Bowling 2; Baseball 2; Hockey 1, 2; Cooperative Council Representative 4.

ELAINE M. MULLOY

23 PARTRIDGE TERRACE, EVERETT

Amiable
Vivacious
A hearty laugh
Prom trotter

Association for Childhood Education 1;
Glee Club 1; Dramatic Club 2; Camera Club
4; *Log* Reporter 2, 3; Cooperative Council
Social Committee 2, Treasurer 3, Representative 2; Outing Committee 4; Assembly Committee Chairman 4; *Clipper* Dance Invitation
Committee 4; Class President 2; Vice-President 3; Fieldball 1, 2; Newcomb 1; Volleyball 1; Baseball 1; Bowling 3; Hockey 1, 2;
Hiking 1, 2; Archery 1; Laurel Chain 3;
New England Regional Convention Delegate
3; President's List 4.

BESSIE NAHIGIAN

53 GOV. WINTHROP ROAD, SOMERVILLE

Friendly
Serene
Quick laughter
"Dark Eyes"

Camera Club 3; Association for Childhood
Education 3, 4; Travel Club 4; Newcomb 1,
2; Volleyball 1, 2, 3; Basketball 1, 3; Hockey
1, 2, 3; Hiking 1, 2, 3; Tennis 1, 2; Fieldball 2; Bowling 2, 3; Soccer 3.

ANNA MARIE O'BRIEN

8 Charles Street, Somerville

Spun gold
Quiet restraint
Determined
Outdoor girl

Glee Club 2; Camera Club 3; Girl Scouts 3;
Travel Club 4; Association for Childhood
Education 4; Tennis 1, 2; Newcomb 1, 2, 3;
Volleyball 1, 2, 3; Hockey 1, 2, 3; Hiking 1,
2, 3; Basketball 1, 3; Fieldball 2; Bowling
2, 3; Soccer 3; President's List 3, 4.

DOROTHY LORETTA PIERS

50 Madison Street, Somerville

Laughing eyes
Dimpled cheeks
A dash of Lily Pons
The epitome of effervescence

Glee Club 1, 2, 3, 4; Association for Childhood Education 3, 4; Junior Prom Refreshment Committee 3; Newcomb 1, Volleyball 1.

LOUISE CURTIS POORE

GARDEN STREET, WEST NEWBURY

Quiet friendliness
Merry chuckle
Twinkling eyes
Sunny disposition

Camera Club 3, 4; Association for Childhood Education 3, 4.

REGINA MARIE POREMBA

136 OTIS STREET, CAMBRIDGE

A ready smile
An easy air
A queenly way
A maiden fair

Glee Club 2, 3; Association for Childhood Education 3, 4; Travel Club 4; Junior Prom Decoration Committee 3; Senior Reception Decoration Committee 4.

DORIS ELEANOR RANDALL

33 Clement Avenue, Peabody

A lover of sports
Pep, vim, vigor
Bubbling brook
A jolly rogue

Camera Club 3; Association for Childhood Education 3, 4; International Relations Club 4; Senior Reception Decoration Committee Chairman 4; Class Executive Board 3, 4; WAA Head of Volleyball 3, Manager of Individual Sports 4; Baseball 1; Fieldball 1, 2; Newcomb 1, 2; Volleyball 1, 2; Bowling 1, 2; Basketball 1, 2, 3; Hockey 1, 2, 3; Hiking 1, 2, 3; Soccer 3, 4.

MARION LOUISE SMITH

705 Broadway, Saugus

A gracious smile
Steadfast
Cooperative
Winter sportster

Glee Club 1, 2, 3; Travel Club 4; Association for Childhood Education 4; Fieldball 1; Volleyball 1; Archery 1; Hiking 1, 2.

HANNAH E. WAITE

68 Bow Street, Lexington

Slender and stylish
Tuneful
Winsome
The Grasshopper's Pilot

Glee Club 1; Craft Club 4; Junior Prom Favor Committee 3; Senior Reception Orchestra Committee 4; Outing Committee 4; Newcomb 2; Volleyball 2; Basketball 2, 3; Hiking 2, 3.

BARBARA WOOD

15 Manning Street, Ipswich

Versatile
Idealistic
Distinguishing poise
"Oh, Johnny, Oh!"

Association for Childhood Education Secretary 1; Dramatic Club 1, Social Chairman 3; Camera Club 4; Outing Committee 4; Class Executive Board 2, 4; Cooperative Council Treasurer 4; WAA Head of Yale 2, 3; *Log* Reporter 2, 3, 4; Fieldball 1, 2; Newcomb 1, 2, 3; Basketball 1, 2, 3, 4; Bowling 1; Hiking 1, 2, 3; Tennis 1; Archery 1; New York Conference 3; Laurel Chain 3; President's List 4.

MARION EVELYN BLANCHARD

33 GORDON STREET, WEST SOMERVILLE

Singer of songs
Super-secretary
Mischievous and merry
But definitely!

Craft Club 4; Class Finance Committee 1; Junior Prom Ticket and Favor Committees 3; WAA Nominating Committee 4; Senior Reception Ticket Committee 4; Class Secretary 1, 2, 3, 4; Newcomb 2, 3; Basketball 2, 3, 4; Volleyball 2, 3, 4.

MARIE BUTLER

4 MASON STREET, SALEM

Placid and patient
Partial to Vincent
Excels in basketball
And have you heard her whistle?

Glee Club 1, 2, 3; Craft Club 4; Junior Prom Favor Committee 3; Senior Reception Committee 4; WAA Nominating Committee 4; WAA Social Committee Chairman 4; Ring Committee 4; WAA Executive Board 4; Hockey Honor Team 1; Fieldball 1; Baseball 2; Honor Basketball Team 1, 2, 3, 4; Newcomb 2, 3, 4; Modern Dancing 2; Volley Ball 2, 3, 4; Class Representative 4; President's List 4.

STELLA MARGARET DOBROW

89 ALLEY STREET, LYNN

Inveterate interrogator
Remarkable manager
Full of pep
Always industrious

Association for Childhood Education 1, 2, 3, 4; Mathematics Club 1, 4, Vice President 2, Publicity Director 3; Council Publicity Committee 3, 4; *Log* News Editor 3, Club Editor 4; Newcomb 1, 2; Basketball 1, 2; Hiking 1.

DENNIS FOLEY

8 GARDEN STREET, NEWBURYPORT

Talented tenor
Reserved expression
Behind which lurks
A subtle humor

Graduate of the Junior High Course, 1936

CATHERINE J. GREENWOOD

5 ENDICOTT AVENUE, BEACHMONT

Capable
Generous
Repeatedly proves herself
Proficient in the profession.

Association for Childhood Education 3, 4.

ANITA H. IRESON

11 JOHNSON STREET, SAUGUS

Cooperative
Clever with a camera
Congenial
A good sport

Association for Childhood Education 1, 4; Camera Club 1, 3, 4, Secretary 2, Maintenance Committee 4; Cooperative Council Publicity Committee 4; Senior Reception Decoration Committee 4; Fieldball 1; Newcomb 1; Volleyball 1; Basketball 1; Tennis 1, 2; Tenikoit 2, 3; Badminton 3; Modern Dance 2; New England Teachers College Preparation Convention Delegate 1; President's List 4.

RAYMOND W. LARSON

57 RYDER AVENUE, MELROSE

Casual genius
Tall
Blond
And indifferent

Camera Club 1, Treasurer 2, President 3, 4; Junior Prom Decoration Committee 3; Senior Reception Decoration Committee 4; *Clipper* Dance Decoration Committee 4; *Clipper* Photography Editor 4; Junior Varsity Basketball 2, 3, 4; Class Day Usher 3; Graduation Usher 3; President's List 4; Commencement Speaker 4.

MARIE LeCOLST

7 CRESCENT STREET, LYNN

Pretty
Pleasingly petite
Unlimited vitality
Forever a fun lover

Dramatic Club 1; Glee Club 2, 3; Craft Club 4; Association for Childhood Education 3, 4; Field Hockey 1, 2; Fieldball 1, 2, 3; Basketball 2; Baseball 2; Volleyball 2, 3; Tennis 1, 2; Archery 1, 2; College Choir 3; New England Teachers Preparation Convention Delegate 4; President's List 4.

FREDERICK LIPMAN

124 Eastern Avenue, Lynn

Loquaciously affable
Man-about-college
The plain varnished truth
Hail-fellow-well-met

Mathematics Club 1, 2, 3; Men's Glee Club 2, 3; Junior Varsity Basketball 1, 2, 3, 4, Manager 2, 3; Varsity Baseball Manager 2, 3, 4; MAA Executive Board 2, 3, 4; President's List 4.

IRENE JOAN MALIK

593 Summer Street, Lynn

Modest
Mild
Musical
Mathematically-minded.

Mathematics Club 1, 2, Vice-President 3, President 4; Association for Childhood Education 1, 2, 4, Secretary 3; *Log* Reporter 3; Basketball 1; Newcomb 1; Hiking 1.

BARNEY MAZONSON

170 BRYANT STREET, MALDEN

Distinguished leadership
Personality plus
The people's choice—
Past, present, and future

Dramatic Club. Membership Committee 3,
Play 3; Camera Club 4; Junior Prom General Chairman 3; Council Nominating Committee 3; *Clipper* Dance Orchestra Committee 4; Class President 3, 4; Men's Glee
Club Vice-President 2; MAA Executive
Board 2; Junior Varsity Basketball 2; Varsity Basketball 3, 4; Varsity Baseball 2;
New England Teachers Preparation Association Conference 3, 4; Students Federation of
America Conference 3; Class Day Usher 3;
Graduation Usher 3; College Choir 3, 4;
President's List 4.

MARGARET McDEVITT

107 WYMAN STREET, LYNN

Efficient
Conscientious
The ever-ready helper
And how she enjoys a joke!

Association for Childhood Education 2,
Treasurer 3, Senior Representative 4; Book
Club Secretary 3; Craft Club Treasurer 4;
Class Finance Committee 1; *Clipper* Dance
Decoration Committee 4; WAA Head of
Baseball 2; *Clipper* Art Staff 4; Fieldball 1;
Field Hockey 1; Newcomb 1; Volleyball 1;
Baseball 2; Class Representative 3; President's List 4.

FRANCIS McINNERNEY

8 MASSACHUSETTS AVENUE, LYNN

Unpredictable
Journalistic volubility
Suitcases, briefcases, bags, stuff
AND a bicycle

Camera Club 1, 2, Treasurer 3, Business Manager 4; Men's Glee Club 1, 2, President 3, 4; Junior Varsity Basketball 3, 4; Track 3; College Choir 3; President's List 4.

DOROTHEA MURPHY

51 AMORY STREET, CAMBRIDGE

Affable
Jovial
A willing worker
And can she jive!

Glee Club 1, 2; International Relations Club 3; Craft Club 4; Association for Childhood Education 1, 2, 3, 4; Class Finance Committee 1; Junior Prom Ticket Committee 3, Class Treasurer 3, 4; Class Vice-President 1, 2; Hockey Honor Team 1; Fieldball 1, 2; Newcomb 1; Volleyball 1; Soccer 1; Archery Honor Team 1; Baseball 1; Tenikoit 1; New England Teachers Preparation Conference Delegate 1, 2, 3.

HELEN M. OSBORNE

48 Luke Road, Everett

Quiet
Unruffled as a rule
Curly-top
A ready laugh

Glee Club 1, 2; Camera Club 3; Association for Childhood Education 1, 2, 3, 4; Craft Club Vice-President 4; Basketball 1; Fieldball 1, 2; Hockey 1, 2; Soccer 1; Baseball 1, 2.

JEANNETTE POLLACK

6 Clarkwood Street, Mattapan

A culinary artist
Indubitably brilliant
A confirmed cynic—
But indispensable

ALICE FRANCES STONEY

3 Fern Street, Lexington

A composer of harmony
A master of crafts
Witty and jolly
Excels in originality

Craft Club 4; Junior Prom Favor Committee Chairman 3; *Clipper* Associate Editor 4; Class Executive Board 4; Senior Reception Ticket Committee 4; Hockey Honor Team 2; Fieldball 2; Basketball 2, 3, 4; Volleyball 2, 3; Newcomb 2, 3; President's List 2, 4; Laurel Chain 3; Class Representative 3.

ROZELDA VERNICK

8 Cliff Street, Salem

Decidedly decorative
A literary leader
Versatile
An asset to any class

Association for Childhood Education 1, 2; Dramatic Club 1, 2, 3, 4; Council Treasurer's Committee 3, 4; Junior Prom Decoration Committee 3; Senior Reception Committee 4; WAA, Head of Dancing 3, Vice-President 4; *Log*, Sports Editor 2, Associate Editor 3, Editor-in-Chief 4; Fieldball 1, 2; Hockey 1, 4, Honor Team 3; Basketball Class Team 1, 2, 3, 4; Newcomb 1, 2; Volleyball 1, 2, 3; Modern Dance 2, 3, 4; Bowling 2; Archery 1, 2, 3; President's List 2, 3, 4; Daisy Chain 3; Columbia Scholastic Press Association Conference Delegate 3.

Classes

Senior Class Officers

2nd Row: A. Stoney, B. Wood, D. Randall, Executive Board; M. Blanchard, Secretary.
1st Row: B. Mazonson, President; R. LaPorte, Vice-President; R. Bath, Treasurer.

SENIOR CLASS ACTIVITIES

October 11	Barn Dance—Decorations and refreshments in the true rural spirit —hay, pumpkins, cider and doughnuts.
April 18	*Clipper* Dance—Spring decorations—apple trees, brown-eyed Susans, gamboling lambs—and *one* black sheep!
June 9	Baccalaureate
June 10	Class Outing
June 11	Class Day
June 12	Commencement Frederick J. Gillis, assistant superintendent of chools in Boston, delivered the commencement address. The invocation was given by the Reverend Milo E. Pearson of Salem
June 12	Senior Reception

Commercial Seniors

4th Row: F. Gilmore, A. Conlon, J. Donahue, J. Sullivan, H. Brenner, H. Baush, R. Batt, J. McKinlay, J. Donegan, S. Finkle, A. Rowsemitt, L. Tripp.

3rd Row: P. DeCoulos, G. Gurin, M. Poirier, K. Sweeney, A. Nelson, Y. Bernardin, M. Kaplan, D. Field, F. Eisenberg, E. Loitman, J. Reed, M. Lefthes.

2nd Row: A. Johnson, M. Marshall, A. Sawyer, R. Norton, M. Hartnett, L. Roderick, M. Kelty, A. Rombult, M. Medeiros, H. Pearlmutter, M. Mooney.

1st Row: B. Hulbert, B. Swan, E. Queenan, A. Boudreau, Mr. Sproul, J. Kochanska, I. Carraher, L. Sideri, M. Fitzgerald.

Most Likely to Succeed
JOSEPH SULLIVAN

Most Studious
ARTHUR BOUDREAU

Most Dignified
YVONNE BERNARDIN

Most Bashful
RUTH NORTON

Most Colorful Personality
KATHRYN SWEENEY

Most Sophisticated
LOUISE SIDERI

Friendliest
BARBARA SWAN

Most Mischievous
HENRY BAUSH

Class Wit
ALBERT CONLON

Most Loquacious
MARY HARTNETT

Junior High Seniors

3rd Row: J. Forte, A. Studentas, F. Drabinowicz, C. Schiorring, S. Prescott, E. Getchell, W. Fine, G. Zoulias.

2nd Row: M. Sutherland, R. LaPorte, R. Keane, R. Pedroni, S. Knowles, L. Watson, R. Levin, H. Hilton, M. Tobin, L. Moulton, R. Prescott.

1st Row: S. Fredman, M. Koroskys, F. Buckley, O. Sapp, Miss Burnham, R. Gallagher, S. Zetes, M. Kincaid, B. Wahl.

Most Likely to Succeed
ALPHONSO SUDENTAS

Most Studious
SHIRLEY KNOWLES

Most Dignified
RUTH LaPORTE

Most Bashful
FRANCIS DRABINOWICZ

Most Colorful Personality
RUTH KEANE

Most Sophisticated
SHIRLEY FREDMAN

Friendliest
CLARA SCHIORRING

Most Mischievous
MARJORIE KINCAID

Class Wit
RUTH LEVIN

Most Loquacious
JOSEPH FORTE

Elementary Senior I

2nd Row: B. Nahigian, H. Waite, L. Poore, R. Poremba, B. Manolakis, R. Cameron, M. Smith, H. Enos.
1st Row: A. O'Brien, D. Randall, R. Cotter, Miss Wallace, R. Cronin, D. Piers.

Most Likely to Succeed
RITA COTTER

Most Studious
ANNA O'BRIEN

Most Dignified
BESSIE NAHIGIAN

Most Bashful
LOUISE POORE

Most Colorful Personality
MARION GRAVES

Most Sophisticated
REGINA POREMBA

Friendliest
HELEN ENOS

Most Mischievous
DORIS RANDALL

Class Wit
DOROTHY PIERS

Most Loquacious
RUTH CRONIN

Elementary Senior II

3rd Row: N. Benkovitz, H. Baldwin, B. Wood, E. Mulloy.
2nd Row: A. Iandoli, F. LeBlanc, H. Kelly, B. Evans, D. Larrabee.
1st Row: H. Esty, B. Miller, Mr. Woods, A. Hayes, M. Baltzer.

Most Likely to Succeed
DOROTHY LARRABEE

Most Studious
NECHAMA BENKOWITZ

Most Dignified
HELEN BALDWIN

Most Bashful
RUTH BROOKS

Most Colorful Personality
ELAINE MULLOY

Most Sophisticated
BARBARA WOOD

Friendliest
BARBARA MILLER

Most Mischievous
AGNES HAYES

Class Wit
AGNES HAYES

Most Loquacious
HELEN KELLY

Special Education Seniors

3rd Row: F. Lipman. B. Mazonson. R. Larson, D. Foley, F. McInnerney.
2nd Row: M. LeColst. M. Blanchard, A. Stoney, Miss Hoff, A. Ireson.
           H. Osborne, J. Pollack, I. Malik.
1st Row: R. Vernick, M. Butler, D. Murphy, C. Greenwood. M. Mc-
           Devitt, S. Dobrow.

Most Likely to Succeed
RAYMOND LARSON

Most Studious
STELLA DOBROW

Most Dignified
MARIE BUTLER

Most Bashful
IRENE MALIK

Most Colorful Personality
BARNEY MAZONSON

Most Sophisticated
ROZELDA VERNICK

Friendliest
ALICE STONEY

Most Mischievous
FRED LIPMAN

Class Wit
DOROTHY MURPHY

Most Loquacious
FRED LIPMAN

Junior Class Officers

2nd Row: R. Clancy, M. Smith.
1st Row: L. Anzuoni, M. Shaw.

JUNIOR CLASS ACTIVITIES

October 27   Football Record Hop—The hall was colorfully decorated with college banners.

May 10   Junior Prom—For the first time in the history of the college, the dance was held away from the college, in the main ballroom of the New Ocean House in Swampscott. Gold lockets and leather key cases were distributed as souvenirs. The affair was acclaimed the greatest social success of the year.

Commercial Juniors

4th Row: E. Pappadopoulos, V. Jonnson, M. Kavanagh, E. Levin, G. Morey, J. Constantinidis, H. Shumrak, D. Fisner, B. Simpson, W. Gibbs.

3rd Row: N. Carpinone, E. Nelson, M. McGarahan, B. Brown, W. Mager, P. Smyrnios, E. Pelley, A. Connick, R. Polansky, A. Heino, A. Rentoumis.

2nd Row: S. Garber, G. Marques, L. Hill, G. Spofford, R. Reynolds, M. Caram, M. Stanley, M. Snaw, M. Shosterman, L. Blood, F. Cirioni.

1st Row: C. Madian, B. Colocousis, B. Hourihan, M. Tarbox, D. Carroll, Mr. Hardy, R. Eynon, E. Eynon, E. Foley, H. Snea, E. Folan.

Junior High Juniors

3rd Row: J. Seigal, R. Beaucage, R. Clancy, M. Smith, D. Parks, J. Attridge, W. Colbert, E. Tedeschi.

2nd Row: H. Hughes, R. McMullen, J. Holloran, M. Holbrook, K. O'-Leary, M. Fossa, L. Anzuoni, G. Malik.

1st Row: J. Herlihy, E. Pirie, E. Chase, M. Thompson, Miss Harris, J. Preston, H. Martin, M. McCarthy V. Witham.

Elementary Junior I

3rd Row: N. Canter, M. McAuliffe, M. Forbes, V. Packard.
2nd Row: A. Timms, E. Ryan, V. Kay, E. Dickson, E. Shepherd.
1st Row: E. Weinstein, M. Locke, Mr. Whitman, A. Riley, E. Johnson,
                 C. Gallant.

Elementary Junior II

3rd Row: D. Lyons, M. Squires, M. Cardinal, P. Johnson, H. Houston.
2nd Row: P. Pitts, A. Quimby, M. Hyman, S. Lobacz, E. Bergman, B. Shaughnessy, H. Rovic.
1st Row: G. Boyle, V. Taylor, Miss Porter, M. Wallace, I. Gagnon, R. Preston.

Sophomore Class Officers

2nd Row: B. Staples, Financial Secretary; L. Newell, Treasurer; H. O'Shea, Secretary.

1st Row: M. Carey, Vice-Prsident; C. Santilli, President.

SOPHOMORE CLASS ACTIVITIES

December 12   Christmas Party. Entertainment was furnished by Santa Claus and members of the class.

April 5   Record Hop—April showers were suggested by umbrellas, rain drops, and blossoming trees. Features included many novelty dances and a quiz by Professor Hay Myser.

April   The adoption of the motto *Semul et Simul* and of the class colors blue and silver.

Commercial Sophomore I

3rd Row :   W. Stanton, A. Anderberg, R. Viens, N. Hymanson, G. Gerrig, M. Chornesky, M. Gradone, P. Godfrey, M. Herman.

2nd Row :   N. Garber, P. Costello, J. Desmond, P. Allen, C. Hallett, E. Donovan, O. D'Ambrosio, J. Bedard.

1st Row :   H. Coffey, G. Cooper, H. Wall, Miss Badger, J. O'Leary, V. Ball, M. Brown, R. Egan.

Commercial Sophomore II

3rd Row: E. Johnson, S. Quigg, J. Hassett, E. Pinder, E. Zeppernick, R. Kelley, M. Watson, V. Wagner, M. McKenna, C. Sullivan

2nd Row: R. Janes, B. Harkins, B. Weinerman, F. Kennis, R. Zaccone, L. Sieve, D. Sakrison, M. Wood, L. Ricciardello, S. Logan.

1st Row: R. Keyes, F. Seymour, M. Twomey, B. Hughes, Miss Edwards, E. Slattery, P. Smith, N. Reynolds, T. LoPorto.

Sophomore I

3rd Row: M. Sullivan, G. McKeeman, C. Crockwell, R. Boyce, M. Seigal, M. Texeira.

2nd Row: M. Traquair, H. Chrisomalis, L. Abelson, M. Folan, H. Brownrigg, M. Gilhooley, P. Donahue, I. Morse.

1st Row: R. DeSimone, V. Rice, Miss Perry, C. Santilli, R. Hill, R. Gallant, M. Nissenbaum.

Sophomore II

3rd Row: E. Litvack, M. Connors, B. Murphy, M. Kiley, M. Myers.
2nd Row: A. Paoli, E. Phelan, V. Green, R. Carney, R. Sack, H. Gallagher, N. Morandi.
1st Row: U. Lombard, L. Gagnon, E. DePaolo, Miss McGlynn, M. Marr. E. Rose, V. Linden, A. Driscoll.

Sophomore III

3rd Row: M. Fargo, M. Mael, G. Stacy, L. Newell, J. Howard, M. Bernstein, M. Bailey, B. Moody, B. Friedman.
2nd Row: A. Cloon, K. Melville, G. Bailey, M. Haverty, H. Locke, W. Dalton, M. Dandeneau, A. McNeil, E. Flynn, I. Senger.
1st Row: M. Carey, M. Halloran, R. Cogswell, Miss Goldsmith, B. Staples, F. Farrell, L. Connolly, M. Cashman.

Freshman Class Officers

2nd Row: S Henderson, Secretary;
P. Roberts, Vice-President;
S. Hankins, Treasurer.
1st Row: C. Kelley, President.

FRESHMAN CLASS ACTIVITIES

December 13
A combination get-together and Christmas party was held in the assembly hall. Solos, dances, and violin selections were given by talented members of the class.

June 10
Annual Freshman outing

Freshman I and II are planning individual yearbooks to record the activities of their first year at college.

Commercial Freshmen

4th Row: N. Guidara, R. Barry, C. Conlon, R. Roberts, W. Welch, J. Hancock, V. Ribaudo, E. Murray, J. O'Shea.

3rd Row: H. Alpers, M. Kierce. E. Thompson, H. Thomas, H. Cummings, R. Toggerson, P. Sloan, C. Fischer, B. Sullivan, R. Ahern, M. McElaney, O. Flanders.

2nd Row: M. Canteloupe, A. Latorella, I. Sharp, A. Pekin, P. McGlynn, M. Sullivan, H. Hederson, L. Dulgarian, C. O'Neil, A. Klubock, R. Hajinlian.

1st Row: V. O'Neil, G. McKenney, E. Freedland, M. Shomo, J. Pineault, M. Langford, Miss Roberts, J. Maciaj, E. Tennenbaum, M. Lenihan, D. Frame, S. Palefsky, L. Blacker.

3rd Row: M. Silver, R. Murano, G. McRae, J. Daley, C. Kelley, R. Fraser, H. Donovan, J. Capone, S. Slavitt.

2nd Row: E. Mattos, H. Shore, M. Conway, M. Connors, M. Fliegel, A. Kimball, A. Clarkin, M. Sarota, N. Dewing.

1st Row: M. Weil, M. Buckley, F. Hosker, M. Carbone, Miss Bunton, J. Murray, E. Thistle, J. Sweeney, D. Plant.

Freshman II

4th Row: Y. Landini, M. Dalakis, E. Pacifici, H. Biggar, H. Cillis, M. Mulligan.

3rd Row: B. McInnes, M. Edwards, G. Hyland, B. McGregor, S. Ring, R. Kelly, E. Lander, M. Gagnon.

2nd Row: M. Miraldi, P. Haley, D. Doane, D. Harding, E. Nestor, D. Eastman, K. McKerrall, E. Milton, E. Paquette.

1st Row: J. McKay, F. Cybush, M. Lovett, S. Hankins, Mrs. King, E. Jackson, M. Glass, A. Donovan, E. O'Brien.

Freshman III

3rd Row: C. Zetes, M. Bluestein, E. Faley, R. Gallant, E. Maloney, R. Rogers, S. Henderson, K. McGillivray, F. Welch, C. Lappas.

2nd Row: J. O'Brien, A. Burwen, B. Flaherty, M. Ciccarelli, N. Smith, B. Thurlow, M. Keegan, H. Busier, M. MacDonald, R. Joyce, M. Welch.

1st Row: C. Scalera, A. Aylward, W. States, D. O'Neil, Miss Stone, V. Durant, M. Dorr, E. Gayton, L. Francis, J. Ragozzino.

Features

Clipper Dance

Commercial History

Off for a new adventure!

Anticipating a thrill-packed voyage, forty-five potential navigators on the seas of commercial pedagogy climbed aboard the training cruiser STATE TEACHERS COLLEGE, anchored at the famous port of Salem, Massachusetts. Recruiting officers all over the State had examined these candidates and had recommended that they be allowed to receive active training duty. This happened in September 1936.

And, as it is recorded in the deck-log, these young hopefuls were greeted by first class petty officers who were to help in orientation. The novices were informed as to what was expected by the line and deck officers and the captain of the ship; they were told that if assignments were carried out from day to day there would be no difficulty in traveling up the ladder to ensign. They learned that each semester would mean an increase in rating. At the end of the first semester they would become seamen third class; the end of the first year would find them seamen second class, and so on until the final increase would lead to a commission as ensign.

In chapel, where these initiates were to learn of many things which cannot be put in words, ideas which would be appreciated later, the voyage was officially begun by a welcome by the captain of the ship. The ropes were cast off. The voyage had begun!

The initial test, aside from the I. Q. examination, was the much dreaded and much talked about initiation. Other than a few minor contusions and abrasions and a few mental upsets, no serious cases were treated as the sick bay. The freshman party, however, helped even up matters.

Soon the routine of answering the roll call, the reporting to the officers of the work done, the occasional shore leave and the sudden squalls and storms (examinations) became part of the day's log. Many of this group of aspirants now found that other specialty fields could be explored. Sports, dramatics, journalism, debating, and a wealth of other groups catered to the abilities of the individual.

Outstanding events during the cruise of that year were the Christmas party, with all the fixings, the trip to the Boston Museum of Fine Arts and the history "answer key," that pamphlet which represented so much frantic and hectic (to say nothing of hectographic) worry and work.

As the season ended the tyros found that they knew how to locate a spot if the angle of the sun, the time of the day and the direction of the shadow were given; they understood the meanings of the "gay" and "kay" looks (no, not anchors), the fundamentals of psychology, the workings and operation of a "mill" (typewriter), and the secrets of science, accounting, and English themes.

But, now we note, as we peruse the ship's log, that the Captain was to retire. Over thirty years of service! A worthy example for the young gobs; and they, conscious of the great work well done, joined with their superiors in bidding farewell.

At the same time, it was farewell to the ship; the summer shore leave was given. And they were now full-fledged seamen second class.

SEPTEMBER 1937

The beginning of the second year! A new captain; a well-trained leader and veteran, in truth, of battles and storms. Shove off!

A year crammed with new and more difficult mooring board problems. Learning how to sell cans of salmon, gloves, hats and suits; working the mills while decoding the cryptic markings taken under fire; discovering the difference between spring and winter wheat; reading history the better to see the future; understanding more about the guidance of those who are to be led and guided when the commission of ensign is conferred—all this happened during the passage.

Furthermore, it was recorded, there was an initiation—this time the newcomers suffered. A new officer in charge of athletics arrived, a Christmas party was held, some went ashore to work during the Christmas shore leave, an inspection was made of Charles River basin, and other points of interest in Boston Harbor. There were a circus and a geography exhibit of New England. It was during this year that the captain's list was established.

And the storms of January and June were met. In January, our voyagers were seamen first class; in June, petty officers third class—half way to the goal. Summer shore leave!

Hurricane!! The cruiser STATE TEACHERS COLLEGE rode gallantly through the storm. Damage was done, but not enough to keep the ship tied up. Anchors aweigh!

A new admiral took over the duties of commissioner; another officer, in charge of languages and law, was added to the roster, while another, in charge of athletics and hygiene, took over the duties of one transfering to another ship.

This year, the sailors receiving commercial pedagogical training began to specialize in either the work of the yeoman or that of the special investigator. However, they were guided and inspired in many of the same classrooms. The mysteries bulk-line cost, the ogive and normal curve, Sedan and Stresa, the Federal Reserve system, the Munroe and Burroughs, annuities, geographical and alphabetical filing, mastery of the facts, and communication, transportation and civil service were revealed during this part of the trip.

A loss which was sincerely mourned by both the enlisted personnel and officers was the death of the officer in charge of bookkeeping.

Of course, in the quick scanning of the pages of the ship's log, it must not be forgotten that many of the commercial group had served on hosts of committees, won honor and distinction in the various specialty clubs, sports and cooperative adventures and had participated in plays, proms and programs.

At the end of the third year it is recorded that forty-two had advanced to the rating of petty officer first class. (Four of the original forty-five had left, while one, who had been ashore on leave, came aboard to complete the journey.) Heigh-ho! No duty until September!

The last year! Get under way!

What ho! A new officer in charge of bookkeeping. Yes, they liked him! And they learned, these sailors, many new things: The party of the first part . . . Dear sir: . . . I move to reconsider the motion . . . the seven cardinal principles . . . Cyrano and his nose . . . the gauge of railways in the United States is four feet, eight and one-half inches . . . the juvenile delinquency . . . line cuts and half tones . . . the sentence method . . . imports and exports . . . the number 2½ pen . . . when teaching basketball . . . push-ups. . . .

Following the mid-year storm and picture posing, it is recorded that the chief petty officers (they had increased their rating, and also their number by one) were assigned to an eight-week period of training aboard other ships in the vicinity, where they were allowed to teach. Hard work, but fun.

Then came the hectic moments . . . finals . . . prom . . . banquet . . . rehearsals ... hymns ... gowns ... baccalaureate ... class outing ·. planting ivy . . . and finally, commencement . . . and a commisison . . . and the farewells and the good wishes for "Smooth sailing."

AARON ROWSEMITT.

Junior Prom 1939

Junior High History

Freshman Frolics

Welcome, Class of 1940

Jury trials for nefarious freshmen—past deeds atoned for by extemporaneous talks, a boxing match, feats of strength, close harmony, etc.

Paint, garlic, and other specialties for the men.

Entertainment by Miss Porter at Barstow Manor

"Go in and out the Window"

Community Sing

Story telling and repartee

Organization of the freshman class—establishment of a precedent

"Banking Tomorrow"

Production of our yearbook *Midshipmite*

Wet sponges

Ink up to the ears

Taste of fish glue

Trips to Forest River Park for snapshots—among other things

Initiation into the Mysteries

Egyptology at the Fine Arts Museum . . . When I was one, I was just begun . . . xylem and phloem . . . elevation of the sun . . . fiction analysis . . . Hammurabi . . . primary addition facts . . . *Joseph Andrews* . . . tropical rain forests . . .

Outing at Canobie Lake

Swimming—and lost accessories!

Roller skating, roller coaster, canoeing—the works!

Real goodfellowship

Sophomore Snaps

Indian Exhibition

Pueblos in the making—clay to the elbows

Bead work

Hand looms

Costume designing—and modeling!

Mount Chocorua

Tears and laughter

Jest and anecdote

Aching joints for two whole days

Practice teaching

Skin the Snake

Highland Schottische

Complications and entanglements

Sophomore Circus

High dive—with overshoes, raincoat, and umbrella

Husky ballet dancers

The mournful clown

A bone-gnawing wild man

The field—near and far

Pioneer Village

Salem Superior Civil Court

State Legislature

Peabody Museum

Essex Institute

Reading Junior High School

Midshipmite II

Squalls at sea

Tombstones and epitaphs

Sketches—realistic and revelatory

Sophomoric Summary

Beowulf . . . uplifted peneplain . . . footnotes . . . bibliographies . . . . . Whan that Aprille with his shoures sote . . . discipline from within . . . sixty day method . . . four stroke cycle . . . forty acres and a mule . . . forty cows and a silo . . .

Junior Gestures

Visit to the gas works—or *Science Triumphant*

White caps

Deafening roars
Excruciating heat
Soot, soot, soot
European Exhibition
"What do you sell that comes from Czechoslovakia?"
"What per cent of the people here are Lithuanian?"
International Institute, Immigration Bureau, foreign quarters
Charts, maps, graphs—and borrowed treasurers
Practice—Teaching
From the known to the unknown
Lesson plans, revised and re-revised
"At last, practice, not theory."
Midshipmite III
Thousands of "portraits"
Stencil cutting
The Mystery of the Missing Styli
Picnic at Crane's Beach
The polka
Cake relays
Sandlot baseball—more sand than ball
Jumbled Impressions
Simultaneous equations . . . *laissez-faire* . . . the neural basis of
learning . . . Penelope's man . . . Flower in the crannied wall . . .
cultural zone A . . . heredity and environment . . . child-centered cur-
riculum . . . Mendel's experiments . . . In Xanadu did Kubla
Khan . . .
Senior Specialties
Literary Pilgrimages
Abe Lincoln in Illinois
The House of Seven Gables
Practice—Teaching
The poise that comes with experience
Surprise and disappointments
Reluctance to return to academic work
Farm Reports
Indomitable inquisitors and perplexed agriculturalists
"Why is your farm where it is?"
"How many cows? Why? Where? What kind?"
Harbor Trip
Elevators, storage tanks, dry dock, ship's cradle
Water wark, cargo, flag, crew
"Note the conflict of land and water traffic."
Fish Pier—slippery scales, fillets, wealth from the briny deep
Watson's Soiree
"Ice Skating is Nice Skating"
Campfire Singing
New England supper
Talented impersonations
Factory Reports
Soap, candy, boxes, shoes, snuff, glue
Raw materials, power, markets, problems
Nature Study Exhibition
"Cuckoo, Who Am I?"
The secret of the rare tropical bird
Ceramic pencils and India ink
Infernal machines and witches' brew
Parties for all occasions
Little Rose Elf materializes
Valentines—sentimental and otherwise
St. Patrick and St. George clasp hands
Bowling—range 114 to 25—quartile deviation?
Basketball Flash
Our valiant lads at the intra-mural semi-finals for the fourth time
ROSELLA GALLAGHER

Foot

Elementary History

"What is it like?" That was one of the questions the family asked after our first day at college. There were sixty different answers in sixty different ways given to that more or less simple inquiry. Some were excited, some enthusiastic, some disappointed, and some non-committal. The same question still holds good, but there are only twenty-eight of us to answer it now. Our first answer was based on impression; our answer today has behind it the experience of four years.

What has it been like aside from the usual classes and studying which one gets in any college? In four years many things can happen and they began happening for us that day in September, 1936, when we came together for the first time to meet each other, our Senior Sisters, our teachers, our faculty advisers, Miss Stone and Miss Rowe, and to sip pink lemonade in the lunch room. Such was the ceremony which launched us on the four year trip we are just completing.

We soon fell into the ritual of alphabetical seating, atetndance books, and quarter-to-four classes. Then rumors began to reach us of fearful doings in the future (a not-too-distant future either), for the time for our so-called official initiation was approaching. As the event called forth a banquet and prizes for table decorations we had a Circus at one table (in more ways than one) and came dressed in our gym suits and wore bows in our hair and carried dolls. At the other table we worked up a most attractive autumn setting.

The actual initiation was not so dreadful as we had been led to believe. Two girls had to link arms and legs and go into a dance; some had to blow cars across the room, other had to give extemporaneous talks on rather amusing subjects, while still others of us landed in the Torture Chamber.

Before we knew it, it was Christmas and the signal was given for our Christmas parties. One game called for the imitation of the poses of the statues in the Hall. As imitators we were no good, especially the one resulting in a most unbalanced "Discus Thrower."

As freshmen we were more athletic than we have ever been since. It seems that we went out for about every sport there was and at the W. A. A. banquet many of us received our athletic awards.

Speaking of banquets, we attended one more before our first year was over. That was in honor of Doctor Pitman who was retiring. The very last fun we had as freshmen was up at Canobie Lake where we went for our class outing. Just to make it more exciting someone had to fall in the lake.

We're all agreed that the outstanding personality of our Sophomore year was Mr. Isadore Isenberg. Miss Wallace and Miss Goldsmith were our advisers, but Miss Goldsmith took a sabbatical leave, and that's where Mr. Isenberg came in. Elementary II were Mr. Isenberg's special charges or "cherubs" as he was wont to call them. As his guests we attended the movies in Revere and dined afterwards. When Miss Goldsmith returned, we had a get-together at Miss Flanders' home in Swampscott.

This was the year that we developed the mania which was something like a subway rush of running upstairs as if a demon were after us with no other purpose in mind except to get the back seats. We filled in a lot of meaningless blanks and argued over the determination of scores. That seems funny now, but then we heartily disagreed with the curve of distribution. Just about this time, too, we began to have mid-years and finals to cope with.

Our Sophomore year was marked by one great sorrow in the death of one whose memory we respect. Just as she shared so many of our experiences then, so she is a part of our story now.

As Juniors we returned to college with hurricane force—to make a bad pun. (Gosh, that was worse than might have been expected.) An important part of that year was the seminars, as we named them, that we used to hold every spare period in that rear left-hand corner of the Chapel Hall. It seems as if we discussed everything under the sun up in that corner and had more fun than a barrel of monkeys.

This Christmas we had our annual parties with our advisers, Miss Bunton and Mr. Woods. Miss Bunton presented each one in her class with a little flower pot containing a sprig of holly. During the vacation we met in Boston for lunch at "The Hideaway" and to see Charles Laughton in *The Beachcomber*. Do you remember how surprised we were when we returned from this vacation to discover that one of the girls had eloped?

By unanimous vote the best part of our Junior year was the last semester. For nine whole weeks we were in training! Can't you still remember your first class? It was an arithmetic class. You may talk all the theory you want, but until you have even a little experience it doesn't mean so very much.

The long-awaited senior year has rolled around at last, and with it another refreshingly-enlightening training period. At least this year started off well. Let's hope it ends just as well.

In the distribution (or should we say presentation) of faculty advisers we were most fortunate. With Miss Wallace and Mr. Woods to give us any assistance we might require, how could we go astray? Evidently the converse doesn't apply, for Mr. Woods hied himself off to the hospital in the middle of winter and the only assistance we could give him was in the form of good wishes.

One afternoon we went to Boston to the theatre to see that most excellent of plays, *Abe Lincoln in Illinois,* starring Raymond Massey. During our February vacation (a week or so after the famous blizzard of 1940) we saw Spencer Tracy in the motion picture version of Kenneth Roberts' *Northwest Passage.*

From the vacation onward we wandered through a maze of class dues, rings, pictures, year book sittings, themes, reports, papers, exams, and a conglomeration of senior responsibilities. "Wandered," for that best describes the impatience we felt with the duties we must perform when all the while our thoughts were on the future we hoped to fashion for ourselves. A future a little fearful to approach, but one which beckoned most enticingly.

That future stretches before us, a future we cannot meet together, but which is for each of us a new and individual undertaking. It is a fascinating ideal, for it embodies all our hopes, our dreams, and our ambitions. It enhances our imagination and acts as the spur to lead us on. May that future see the fulfillment and the realization of those things of which you've dreamed these past years.

RITA COTTER.

Class Day 1939

Special Education History

They laughed when a student leading chapel one morning accidently referred to us as the "Social Eds." They didn't know until later that a more suitable title for our illustrious group would be difficult to find. All work and no play is definitely not our motto. In strict accordance with our course, we have a recipe instead of a motto to suit our purpose.

Take five days of hard work. Add a generous supply of jokes with a pinch of puns. Garnish with a dash of good humor, unlimited cooperation, and good will. Simmer slowly for one week and serve hot on the third floor. The result, one week of well-rounded activity.

Much of our time is occupied with the study of the Psychology of the Feeble-minded. We deviate from the usual path of education however, when the men don aprons for cooking or take up the gentle art of needlework and when the women are given an opportunity to wield the hammer. Our experiments in science sometimes have spectacular results and our craftwork is beyond description.

We have become so conscious of I. Q.'s that our table at the Initiation Banquet was decorated with such a theme in mind. The center piece was Charlie McCarthy. The tablecloth resembled a huge Intelligence Test, while our members donned dunce caps—just for the occasion, of course.

And it must be admitted that we do have a little semblance of prestige. We are proud to acknowledge that among our members we have several people prominent in school affairs, among them the President and Secretary of the Senior Class as well as one other member of the Executive Board, the Editor-in-Chief of the *Log*, two members of the *Clipper* Staff, the President of the Math. Club, the President of the Camera Club, and the Chairman of the W. A. A. Social Committee, not forgetting, of course, half the Grasshopper Sextet.

The Special Education social season opened with a gala Hallowe'en Party held in Miss Walker's room in the Training School. Special entertainment and extra special refreshments were provided for us by the pupils of the Special Class The next event of note was the party given on the third floor in honor of Miss Hoff's birthday. The room just across the hall from the Art room was the scene of another gay affair in December. At this time Christmas was celebrated in true Special Ed. fashion with joke presents for all and refreshments galore. Early in February, we attended a Skating Party sponsored by Miss Walker's class. Many of us donned ski suits and spent a memorable afternoon showing our skill (or the opposite) on skates.

On February 16th, the time had arrived for us to temporarily relinquish our role of students. We stepped out into the world, leaving the sacred walls of S. T. C. behind us, to acquire the title of teachers. Eight weeks elapsed with the members of our group working furiously in widely-scattered communities.

A resume of the big events of the year cannot be satisfactorily concluded, however, without mentioning the two informal get-togethers held during our training period. On March 19th, we were royally entertained by Mr. and Mrs. Little and on April 9th, a similar affair took place at the home of Rozelda Vernick. Here we shared our training experiences and narrated incidents both tragic and humorous.

On April 21st, we once more entered the doors of S. T. C. as a body and resumed the role of students. With training a thing of the past, we earnestly settled down to our knitting—literally and figuratively speaking—and we are back to normal (?) again.

ALICE STONEY.

Class Ode

I

Spirit of song, clear-eyed and grave,
  Thou to whom poets cry for words
To touch men's hearts
  And make them glow
With the same fire they feel.
  Thou from whose lips drops magic
That can make Troy live again,
  And Caesar speak, and Virgil sing,
Down centuries and centuries of time.
  Forever, those who write
Have called, will call upon you,
  When they would speak
In words of singing flame
  Of great achievement or adventuring.
Grant now strong words, yet gentle, too,
  That we may keep in years to come
A memory of worth and dignity,
  And dreams to light the way that we must find.

II

The years run by so swiftly,
  Glide into the secret mantle of the past
So silently, we scarcely sense that they are gone,
  Until one day we stop and look behind
To ask, a little doubtfully,
  What we have done or said
That shall outlive us,
  Abide even when we shall be gone.
What we termed treasure turns to jest
  When the white light of truth
Is turned upon it,
  A poor joke that life played on us,
While, careless in our youth, we laughed,
  Memory can be so cruel!
But still behind our tears
  A voice cries out, and will not be denied,
"You sought for what you knew not, then,
  You lavished all your strength in search
For understanding, not in one way alone,
  Some sought for her in books,
Some in the eyes of friendship,
  Still others in the peace of solitude.
Each true to his beliefs,
  Knowing that peace comes only
To him who is true.

III

And now our nights of endless toil are ended,
  The goal we sought for four long years is won.
What is to come we have no way to know.
  A kind fate hides the future from our view.
One thing alone is certain:
  It shall not greater be nor less
Than we have tried to make the past.
  What we achieve shall be the measure
Of all the achievement we have ever made.

IV

How many times our courage has been tested!
  How many times we failed, but from defeat

Took new encouragement, and fought our way
Back to try once again, and that time, win!
We shall have great need of that courage,
When we shall look upon a world gone mad.
Courage enough to hate the wrong about us,
Courage enough to speak for what is right,
For the old, simple truths that shall endure
When the last warrior has perished by the sword.

V

Men tell us that Democracy is doomed,
That it will die of its own indolence.
With it, we know, will die the freedom
That we have cherished for so many years.
The right to think and speak as we see fit,
To hold our heads erect, to walk with pride,
To seek our happiness in our own way.

VI

There lies our task: to see that this
The best that man has done
For fellow man, has not been done in vain.
To guard the heritage that has been given
To us, with the solemn charge
That we should cherish it,
And keep it safe,
Then, hand it on, a little better,
To the generations that should follow us.
Never forget! lWe are Democracy,
And only if we fail •
Shall its name perish from the earth!

VII

We shall be teachers, not of minds but hearts,
On us the two-fold duty shall descend.
To impart knowledge wil not be enough
We must build character so well
That it shall stand
When everything shall fall.
We must teach love and human brotherhood
And teach them in a world of war and hate;
Preach honesty and courage
In the midst of lies and fear.

VIII

This is our challenge!
This shall be the answer,
To the long years of patient preparation.
To the endless days and nights of work and study:
When we go forth, to catch
The bright, torn banner of Democracy
From hands too tired any longer to support it.
We consecrate to humankind
Our strength, our courage,
All we have to give,
That not because of us,
Shall truth and freedom
Perish from the earth.

——MARGARET SUTHERLAND

Senior Superlatives

Most Likely to Succeed..JOSEPH SULLIVAN

Most Studious .... ARTHUR BOUDREAU

Most Dignified .... RUTH LaPORTE

Most Bashful .... RUTH BROOKS

Most Colorful Personality.......................................KATHRYN SWEENEY

Most Sophisticated .... LOUISE SIDERI

Friendliest...BARBARA·SWAN

Most Mischievous .... JOSEPH FORTE

Class Wit .... FRANCIS McINNERNEY

Most Loquacious .... RUTH LEVIN

Done Most for Class .... BARNEY MAZONSON

Best Looking Girl..AGNES HAYES

Best Looking Boy .... JAMES McKINLAY

Most Athletic Girl .... MARY HARTNET

Most Athletic Boy .... HERBERT BRENNER

Most Carefree .... FRANCIS GILMORE

Most Ambitious .... ALPHONSO SUDENTAS

Most Original .... ALICE STONEY

Most Versatile .... JOSEPH SULLIVAN

Most Literary .... LOUISE MOULTON

Most Musical .... HOPE HILTON

Most Artistic .... BESSIE MANOLAKIS

Most Intellectual .... LOUISE MOULTON

Most Energetic .... RUTH KEANE

Most Idealistic..JOSEPHINE KOCHANSKA
                                                                    MARGARET SUTHERLAND

Organizations

Cooperative Council

3rd Row: R. Pedroni, K. Sweeney, A. Conlon, J. McKinlay, G. Morey, J. Daley, A. Boudreau, E. Jackson, S. Henderson

2nd Row: O. Sapp, R. Gallagher, D. Fischer, R. Keane, M. Langford, E. Slattery, B. Staples, B. Miller, M. Thompson

1st Row: R. LaPorte, E. Mulloy, J. Sullivan, Miss Bell, President Sullivan, Miss Wallace, R. Levin, B. Wood, W. Gibbs

COOPERATIVE COUNCIL ACTIVITIES

September   Establishment of a second-hand book store which, under the management of John Donahue and William Gibbs, handled $50 worth of books.

October 6   Annual Initiation—After the banquet in the college gymnasium, the freshmen were entertained in an unforgettable manner.

November 17   New England Teachers Preparation Association Conferenc.e. Delegates included the Council officers, class representatives, Richard Clancy, Ruth Keane, Aaron Rowsemitt, and Rozelda Vernick.

February   Election for the year 1940-1941. The new officers are President, William Gibbs,; Vice-President, Ruth Cogswell; Secretary, Kathleen O'Leary; and Treasurer, Esther Slattery.

March 8   Council Dance Decorations comprised an underwater scene of Neptune's Palace. During the evening Neptune and his court were chosen.

April 4-6   New York Conference—Richard Clancy, George Morey, Ruth Cogswell, and Margaret O'Shea were the student delegates. They covered the panels: "The Guidance We Need," "How Can We Develop Student Leadership," "How Can We Improve Our College Publications?", and "The Character and Significance of General Programs for the Entire College." Miss Wallace was the faculty delegate to the Conference.

The Clipper Staff

3rd Row: S. Finkle, E. Getchell, M. Poirier, R. Larson, Y. Bernardin,
A. Boudreau, J. Donahue, L. Tripp
2nd Row: B. Swan, A. Stoney, M. Hartnett, R. Cotter, H. Baldwin, D.
Larrabee, H. Enos, A. Johnson
1st Row: R. Gallagher, B. Miller, Miss Perry, L. Moulton, Miss Burnham, P .DeCoulos, M. Sutherland

Clipper Staff

Editor-in-Chief
Louise Moulton

Assistant Editor
Yvonne Bernardin

Associate Editors
Angie Johnson
Rosella Gallagher
Rita Cotter
Barbara Miller
Alice Stoney

Business Managers
Mary Hartnett
Samuel Finkle

Advertising Managers
Arthur Boudreau
John Donahue

Photography Editors
Ellsworth Getchell
Raymond Larson

Literary Editors
Margaret Sutherland
Barbara Swan

Art Editor
Dorothy Larrabee

Art Staff
Helen Baldwin
Ruth Brooks
Helen Enos
Margaret McDevitt

Staff Secretaries
Penelope DeCoulos
Muriel Poirier
Lloyd Tripp

Typists
Winifred Mager
Athena Rentoumis
Ruth Reynolds
Sylvia Prescott

Faculty Advisers
President Sullivan
Miss Burnham
Miss Perry
Mr. Rockett

College Choir

E. Freedland, M. Thompson, R. Prescott, R. LaPorte, F. LeBlanc, B. McInnes, R. Keane, B. Moody, G. Morey, C. Conlon, H. Hilton (pianist).

Commercial Council

3rd Row: M. Stanley, J. O'Shea, B. Hughes
2nd Row: M. Lenihan, S. Palefsky, V. Johnson, M. Fitzgerald, P. Smith
1st Row: J. O'Leary, Secretary; B. Hulbert, President; Mr. Sproul,
               D. Fischer, Treasurer; H. Baush.

COMMERCIAL COUNCIL ACTIVITIES

September-June	Management of the candy counter, the profits of which benefit the entire student body.
November 21	The film "Safari on Wheels" was procured for the entire student body, as well as educational pictures for the geography department.
November 25	New England Commercial High School Teachers Convention —Preparation for this convention, which was held at the college, was the first big undertaking of the council this year.
December 14	Annual Christmas Party—Entertainment by talented members, followed by a community sing.
March 25-29	National Business Show at Mechanics Building, Boston. The Council obtained and distributed over one hundred tickets to the faculty and students.
May 16	Annual Banquet at which Mr. Theodore W. Zeigler spoke on aptitude tests for employment and Mr. Marshall W. Hunt of Lynn exhibited a film entitled "Credit"—The Life of Business."

Association for Childhood Education
Salem Teachers College Branch

4th Row: A. Hayes, R. Joyce, M. Casman, D. Larrabee, M. Lovett, B. Nahigian, H. Esty, I. Malik, M. Holloran, R. Hill, J. Preston

3rd Row: M. Gilhooly, M. Edwards, R. Cotter, B. Evans, H. Houston, R. Poremba, L. Poore, H. Baldwin, M. McAuliffe, M. Smith

2nd Row: D. Randall, H. O'Shea, P. Donahue, H. Cameron, L. Waldron, S. Lobacz, A. Quimby, H. Kelly, R. Cronin, A. O'Brien, L. Flynn, B. Nestor

1st Row: E. Gayton, B. Miller, A. Aylward, M. O'Shea, Secretary; E. Pike, Treasurer; Miss Bunton, M. Squires, President; P. Pitts, A. Riley, D. Piers

Association for Childhood Education Activities

October   Visit to the Children's Museum at Jamaica Plain.
Small group of members attended a meeting of the North Shore Branch in Lynn, at which Dr. Beryl Parker of New York University spoke.

November   Talk on industrial arts followed by a laboratory period of work with clay.

December   Lecture on "Relationship of Parents and Teachers" by Miss Marenda Prentiss of the Massachusetts Child Council.
Lecture by Mr. Orin Skinner at a meeting of the North Shore Branch in Marblehead.

January   Lecture by Miss Katherine Burk, principal of the Aborn School, Lynn—"Characteristics of a Good Teacher'."

February   Miss Sibyl Tucker of the Training School displayed her doll collection and spoke on "Hobbies."

March   The North Shore Branch was entertained at a tea at which Miss Gertrude B. Goldsmith spoke on "Arts and Crafts in Mexico." Mr. George Murphy, supervisor of music in Salem, accompanied the talk with Mexican music.

May   May Party for the eighth grade girls of the Horace Mann Training

Book Club

2nd Row: A. Paoli, R. McMullen, L. Sieve, M. Silver, Miss Harris, H.
           Houston, S. Lobacz, E. Flynn.
1st Row: L. Sideri, M. Mooney, H. Martin, Secretary; Y. Bernardin,
           Vice-President; M. Tobin, President; S. Fredman, Treasurer;
           M. McCarthy, E. Dodge, D. Carroll.

Book Club Activities

General Activities: Book reviews, reports on what America is reading, reading of short stories, and quiz programs on recent fiction, drama, and poetry.

November 2 Visit to Boston *Herald* Book Fair—Lin Yutang showed how he finds humor and beauty in everyday life.

April 25 Book Reviews by Miss Lillian Abbott of the Salem Public Library. Camera, Craft, Dramatic, and Travel Clubs were guests.

April 26 Theater Party.

May 9 Farewell Party.

Camera Club

3rd Row: R. Joyce, E. Tenenbaum, E. Mazonson, J. Hancock, W. Welch, W. Fine, G. Murray, P. McGlynn.

2nd Row: A. Aylward, A. Johnson, V. Ball, M. Traquair, L. Poore, A. A. Ireson, G. Gerrig, F. Eisenberg, P. DeCoulos, M. Koroskys.

1st Row: H. Locke, Vice-President; M. Kincaid, Business Manager; A. Anderberg, Secretary; R. Larson, Co-President; Mr. Whitman, E. Getchell, Co-President; M. Fargo, Treasurer; F. Buckley, F. McInnerney.

Camera Club Activities

General activities open to all members: taking pictures, developing and printing pictures, enlarging, and copying pictures.

October 26   Mr. Whitney gave an illustrated talk on picture composition.

November 9   Demonstration by Mr. Getcrell of how to develop and print pictures.

November 22   Mr. Whitman demonstrated sillouette making.

December 7   Mathematics Club entertained with a quiz contest.

January 4   Demonstration of picture enlarging by Mr. Larson.

February 1   Mr. Lawrence P. Bliss gave an illustrated talk, "It's Great To Be an American." Commercial Council, Book Club, Craft Club, and Travel Club were guests.

March 14   Reverend Elmer Eddy gave an illustrated lecture on the taking of color pictures.

March 28   Demonstration of picture copying by Miss Kincaid.

April 25   Talk on the use of filters by Mr. Fine.

Craft Club

2nd Row: A. Cloon, I. Senger, M. Myers, B. Friedman, E. O'Brien, V. Green.
1st Row: M. Hyde, B. Miller, President; Miss Perry, H. Esty, Secretary; V. Linden.

Craft Club Activities

November—Miss Bartlett from Fellow Crafters demonstrated the possibilities of such hobbies as weaving, metalcraft, leathercraft, blockprinting, and woodcarving.

The members, working independently at the crafts in which they are interested, have made dolls, blockprints, footstools, pins, belts, bracelets, and bookends. They have learned not only interesting hobbies, but also valuable skills for teaching.

Girl's Glee Club

4th Row: E. Freedland, J. McKay, D. Eastman, A. Hayes, G. Boyle, P. Haley, B. Evans, M. Thompson, H. Shore, B. McInnes, M. Cicarelli, G. Cooper, E. Pike.

3rd Row: V. O'Neil, E. Johnson, D. Lyons, K. McKerrall, M. Squires, A. Rombult, A. Kimball, M. O'Shea, F. Welsh, M. Cardinal, P. Johnson, M. McAuliffe, H. Kelly, B. Shaughnessy, M. Marr, J. Murray.

2nd Row: A. Riley, B. Turlow, R. LaPorte, B. Moody, I. Senger, E. Jackson, Mr. Woods, C. Schiorring, M. Dandeneau, R. Keane, F. LeBlanc, A. Clarkin, E. Mattos ,E. Rose.

1st Row: D. Piers, E. Gayton, H. Hilton, Accompanist; S. Zetes, Secretary; R. Pedroni, Vice-President; R. Prescott, President; L. Moulton, Treasurer; R. Cogswell, Librarian; L. Flynn, D. Plant, D. Frame.

Girl's Glee Club Activities

September 28   Initiation Party—Solos, quartets, and community singing. Ingenious new members represented song titles by costume and pantomime.

December 8   Pops Concert—In a gay candle-lit cabaret setting, choral selections, both classical and light, were sung by the club and by "The Singing Men" under the direction of Mr. Woods. Guest artists were Mrs. Ruth Balsom Brown and Mrs. Irene Harris.

December 12   Radio program of Christmas music

May 9   Chapel Program

May 16   Farewell Banquet

International Relations Club

3rd Row: J. Lane, F. Drabinowicz, A. Boudreau, J. Donahue.
2nd Row: F. Cirioni, B. Wahl, A. Connick, A. Heino, D. Randall, E. Foley.
1st Row: O. Sapp, M. Sutherland, President; M. Herman, Vice-President; Miss Cruttenden, N. Carpinone, Secretary-Treasurer; R. Gallagher.

International Relations Club

November 30 and December 1	Conference at New Haven Teachers College Delegates: John Donahue and Maurice Herman
December 8	Christmas Party
December 12	Lecture by Anton J. DeHaas of Harvard Panel Discussions over Station WESX, Salem
January 9	Democracy in the Far East Margaret Sutherland, Nettie Carpinone, Elizabeth Foley, Rosella Gallagher, Olga Sapp
January 23	Pan-Americanism Bertha Wahl, Alice Connick, Elizabeth Foley, Anne Heino, Doris Randall
February 13	Democracy in the Balkans Florence Cirioni, Maurice Herman, Joan Lane, Ruth Levin
March 12	Peace Plans Olga Sapp, Nettie Carpinone, Alice Connick, Rosella Gallagher, Elizabeth Foley, Doris Randall, Margaret Sutherland
March 25	Panel Discussion at First Baptist Church, Beverly Peace Plans Margaret Sutherland, Nettie Carpinone, Elizabeth Foley Rosella Gallagher, Doris Randall, Maurice Smith
April 11	Farewell program for seniors given by undergraduates
April 24	Banquet at Woodberry Tavern, Beverly

John Burroughs Club

2nd Row: E. Faiey, R. Murano, R. Biddell, M. Bernstein, D. O'Neil,
E. Maloney, M. Seigal, S. Slavitt, G. Zoulias
1st Row: L. Anzuoni, E. Pacifici, M. Holbrook, Treasurer; C. Santilli,
Vice-President; Miss Goldsmith, J. Forte, President; E. De
Paolo, Secretary; V. Durant, Executive Board; C. Scopa

John Burroughs Club Activities

September-May   Field trips, illustrated lectures, nature handicraft, and student programs and discussions stimulate enthusiasm, broaden one's concepts, and awaken one to the realization of numerous activities of which the average person knows little.

January 28   Annual meeting of the Audubon Society in Boston.

February 24,
March 2,
March 9   Annual lecture series sponsored by the Audubon Society. Several delegates represented the club at the lectures and at the annual meeting.

April 22   Lecture on hummingbirds by Mr. Laurence B. Fletcher.

May   Visit to the Museum of Natural History in Boston and to the Arnold Arboretum in Cambridge.

Literary—Dramatic Club

4th Row: R. Fraser, S. Finkle, M. Chornesky. P. Roberts, H. Donovan, H. Brenner, J. Howard, B. Mazonson, J. Sullivan, H. Shumrak. J. Constantinidis, W. Gibbs, J. McKinlay

3rd Row: G. McRae, M. Shomo, M. Connors, H. Thomas, K. Sweeney, E. Pelley, M. Folan, E. Sullivan, H. Brownrigg, H. Rovic, S. Garber, E. Thistle

2nd Row: L. Tripp, A. Latorella, M. Carbone, L. Roderick, V. Maciaj, R. Polansky, M. Edwards, R. Toggerson, R. Ahearn. M. Shosterman, G. Marques, M. Hartnett, P. Allen, M. Kierce. N. Hymanson.

1st Row: H. Cillis, E. Nestor, M. Casiman, I. Gagnon, S. Prescott, Vice-President; Mr. Hardy, E. Dickson, President; J. Bedard, G. McKinney, M. Sullivan, M. Holloran

Literary-Dramatic Club

November 1
Initiation Banquet—designed to welcome back old members and introduce new members. Mrs. Rose Gordon gave an entertaining lecture on stage make-up.

November 15
Tournament Plays—The Seniors presented a tragedy, *Lights Out*. The Juniors put on *Night Falls on Spain*, and the Freshmen and Sophomores combined efforts to produce the winning play, *It Pays to be Clumsy*.

December 15
Christmas Play—a major triumph in Dickens' immortal "Christmas Carol." Pupils from the Training School aided an unsually able cast.

March 13
Three Act Play—*The Barretts*—the romantic story of Elizabeth Barrett and Robert Browning (played by Helen Royle and James McKinlay.)

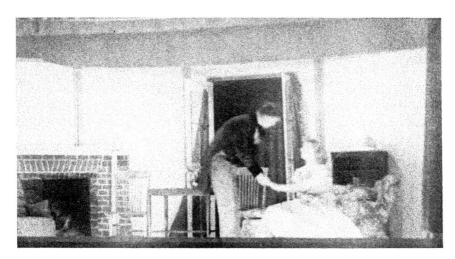

The Log Staff

4th Row: A. Sudentas, E. Thistle, H. Shumrak, J. Howard, J. Donahue,
           G. McRae, J. Attridge
3rd Row: P. DeCoulos, H. Thomas, R. Keane, R. Polansky, E. Levin,
           Y. Bernardin, B. Brown, J. Holloran, H. Rovic, M. Thompson
2nd Row: A. Johnson, L. Huttula, G. Cooper, P. Donahue, P. Allen,
           P. Godfrey, R. Egan, U. Lombard, M. Weil, D. Carroll
1st Row: M. Hartnett, B. Simpson, J. Preston, A. Rowsemitt, Miss
           Edwards, R. Vernick, Miss Porter, R. Bath, F Buckley, L.
           Waldron

Log Activities

November 10   *The Log* Semi-Formal Dance—based on the journalistic theme "Great Events in November." Proceeds used to send delegates to the Columbia Press Conference.

November 16   Massachusetts State Teachers College Publications Association Conference—Fifteen members of the staff traveled to Fitchburg to confer with student journalists of four other teachers colleges. Reverend William T. Murphy, Jr. of Lynn spoke on "Perseverance, Enthusiasm, Power."

March 14, 15, 16   New York Convention of thee Columbia Scholastic Press Association—First class rating in the division of schools of education newspapers went to the *Log*, the only New England paper to achieve this honor.

April 5   M. S. T. C. P. A. Conference at Bridgewater — Six members of the staff heard addresses on factors in news reporting and on making a newspaper pay.

Mathematics Club

3rd Row: R. Boyce, I. Mrose, G. Bailey, H. Hughes. M. Haverty, S. Henderson, M. Bailey, M. Fossa, M. Kavanagh, P. Donahue, M. Dorr, C. Crockwell

2nd Row: M. Fliegel, E. Pacquette, A. McNeil, S. Dobrow, V. Johnson, E. Phelan, M. Carey, M. Kiley, R. Hill, F. Farrell, K. Melville, G. McKeeman

1st Row: J. Ragozzino, L. Connelly, E. Pirie, R. Beaucage, Treasurer; G. Malik, Publicity Director; Miss Stone, I. Malik, President; K. O'Leary, Secretary; J. Attridge, Vice-President; J. Herlihy, J. O'Brien

Mathematics Club Activities

Oct. 19   Visit to the Lynn Credit Bureau where information was received as to how retailers are supplied with material concerning the character of credit customers.

Nov. 23   Annual dinner meeting with Rev. Emerson Schwenk as guest speaker. He told of the history and development of the Consumer Cooperative movement.

Dec. 8   Christmas party that took the form of a quiz contest with the Camera Club as guests and opponents.

Jan. 4   The publication of data concerning motion picture attendance, etc. as as compiled from a survey of the entire student body.

Jan. 11   Annual Amateur Show.

Feb. 1   Miss Louise B. Drew spoke on the "HOWS AND WHYS OF THE HOSIERY PROBLEM."

April 25   Annual banquet with Miss Helen Piper, supervisor of elementary grades in the Lynn schools, as guest speaker.

Pitman Debating Society

3rd Row: J. Attridge, C. Santilli, J. Howard, R. Barry, W. Dalton
2nd Row: P. Donahue, B. Weinerman, A. Latorella, H. Thomas, L.
            Waldron, G. Marques, P. McGlynn, R. Ahearn
1st Row: M. Carbone, M. Twomey, V. Witham, R. Gallagher, Miss
            McGlynn, E. Chase, Vice-President; N. Carpinone, E. Dono-
            van

Debating Club Activities

November 1, 2	Tour to Vermont and New Hampshire University of Vermont Middlebury College for Women	
November 16	Roosevelt Administration—at Worcester College of the Holy Cross	Lost
November 24	Sponsoring of Declamation Contest Winner—Nick Guidara	
December 14	Radio Debate—Isolation Question Middlebury College for Women	Won
December 15	At Woburn—Isolation Question Boston College (Marquette)	Lost
December 19	Radio Debate—Isolation Question Boston College	Won
January 12	At Salem—Isolation Question Boston College (Fulton)	Won
January 30	Radio Debate—Fitchburg Teachers College	Won
February 6	At Salem—Third Term Question College of the Holy Cross	Won
February 6	Radio Debate—Third Term Question College of the Holy Cross	Lost
March 20	Radio Debate—German-Russian Alliance Boston University	Won
Apirl 5	First meeting with Bay Path Institute of Springfield at Salem—Railroad Question	
April 11	Radio Debate—Isolation Question Harvard University	Lost
May 20	Return Debate with Bay Path Institute of Springfield —Isolation Question	

Travel Club

3rd Row :   R. Cronin, N. Benkovitz, H. Baldwin, B. Manolakis, M. Kaplan, M. Poirier, J. Reed, K. Medeiros.

2nd Row :   H. Enos, B. Nahigian, M. Smith, D. Larrabee, H. Cameron, H. Chrisomalis, A. Iandoli, A. O'Brien.

1st Row :   M. Baltzer, R. Cotter, G. Gurin, M. Lefthes, Miss Ware, R. Poremba, M. Nissenbaum, R. DeSimone

Travel Club

November	Visit to the House of Seven Gables, the Coastguard Station, and historic Chestnut Street.
December	International Supper—Food with an accent! Caviar from Russia, cheese from Holland, fish and chips from England, sardines from Norway.
February	Visit to the Agassiz, Peabody, Fogg Art, and Germanic Museums.
March	Lecture on the Isle of Man, England, Mexico, and southwestern United States by Silvie Hankins. Visit to Boston— Custom House, Bunker Hill, Faneuil Hall, King's Chapel, scene of Boston Massacre.
April	Lecture by Miss Margaret L. Galvin of the Perkins Institute for the Blind. Visit to the Gardner Museum in Boston.

Tri Mu

4th Row: R. Janes, F. Seymour, M. Tarbox, H. Shea, H. Coffey, V. Johnson, A. Heino, O. Flanders, D. Fischer, B. Harkins, C. Hallett, F. Cirioni, J. Bedard.

3rd Row: M. Lefthes, D. Sakrison, J. Reed, E. Zeppernick, E. Johnson, M. Poirier, E. Levin, M Watson, A Connick, J. Hassett, E. Nelson, R. Reynolds, H. Thomas.

2nd Row: M. Twomey, R. Keane, P. Godfrey, A. Rombult, R. LaPorte, L. Waldron, L. Hill, E. Slattery, M. Kavanagh, R. Egan, H. O'Shea, P. Allen, A. Rentoumis.

1st Row: C. O'Neil, R. Eynon, E. Eynon, J. Preston, L. Huttula, W. Mager, President; Miss Roberts, B. Hughes, Secretary; L. Francis, P. DeCoulos, B. Hulbert, B. Hourihan.

Tri Mu Activities

Sept. 25 Opening meeting of the Tri Mu for 1939-1940. The club held a weenie roast at Lynn Beach, after which the freshmen and new members were initiated.

Oct. 25 The meeting was held at Weber's. After the business meeting the members left on a scavenger hunt. Prizes were awarded to the winning group and refreshments were served.

Nov. 22 Carolyn Aivezi was hostess to the Tri Mu at her home in Marblehead. After the business meeting, games and refreshments were enjoyed.

Dec. 7 The annual informal dance of the Tri Mu was held in the college gym. Besides dancing, the members and guests enjoyed games and refreshments.

Mar. 4 A bowling party was held at the Lafayette St. alleys, after which refreshments were served at Miss Roberts' apartment.

Mar. 28 The regular March meeting was held at the home of Elenor Levin in Salem. Various games were played and refreshments were served.

Apr. 13 The members attended a matinee performance of "The Hot Mikado" with Bill Robinson at the Shubert Theatre in Boston.

May The closing meeting at Lynn Beach. The memebers cooked a supper out of doors and played games.

M. A. A. and Men's Glee Club

6th Row: W. Colbert, N. Guidara, C. Crockwell, R. Beaucage, J. Constantinidis, J. Daley, F. Drabinowicz, F. Hosker, A. Sudentas, D. Parks, J. Pineault, W. Gibbs, H. Shumrak, N. Hymanson, M. Gradone, R. Viens, S. Sylvia.

5th Row: F. Gilmore, A. Boudreau, R. Biddell, M. Bernstein, J. Donahue, R. Bath, R. Clancy, C. Conlon, B. Mazonson, J. O'Leary, H. Donovan, R. Fraser, P. Smyrnios, J. Lane, M. Seigal.

4th Row: G. Murray, E. Getchell, W. Fine, D. O'Neil, J. Howard, R. Larson, G. Morey, H. Baush, E. Maloney, P. Roberts, W. Welch, C. Kelley, J. Donegan, R. Gallant, N. Lynch.

3rd Row: W. Dalton, S. Slavitt, R. Murano, M. Seigal, C. Santilli, T. Reddy, M. Chornesky, J. Sullivan, J. Hancock, J. Capone, R. Sheehan, R. Boyce, E. Thistle, G. Zoulias, L. Lospennato.

2nd Row: E. Pappadopoulos, C. Zetes, F. Lipman, H. Brenner, Mr. Lowry, A. Conlon, Mr. Woods, J. McKinlay, M. Smith, G. Forte, S. Finkle, L. Tripp.

1st Row: H Locke, G. McKeeman, W. Stanton, C. Lappas, M. Herman, J. Attridge, A. Rowsemitt, N. Fliegel, E. Tenenbaum, J. O'Shea, G. McRae, E. Tedeschi.

Athletics

W. A. A. Executive Board

3rd Row: L. Flynn, M. Carey, M. Finn, J. Bedard, D. Randall.
2nd Row: E. Nelson, R. Pedroni, M. Squires, W. Mager, S. Prescott, R. Reynolds, M. O'Shea.
1st Row: R. LaPorte, E. DePaolo, Mrs. King, R. Keane, R. Vernick, Miss Wallace, A. Sawyer, K. O'Leary.

President
RUTH KEANE

Vice-President
ROZELDA VERNICK

Secretary
ALICE SAWYER

Treasurer
RUTH LaPORTE

Recording Secretary
KATHLEEN O'LEARY

Manager of Team Sports
ELEANOR CHASE

Manager of Individual Sports
DORIS RANDALL

Head of Soccer
MARY FINN

Head of Field Hockey
ELENA DePAOLO

Head of Basketball
RENA PEDRONI

Head of Bowling
EVELYN NELSON

Head of Softball
RUTH REYNOLDS

Head of Volley Ball
LORRAINE FLYNN

Head of Dancing
SYLVIA PRESCOTT

Head of Hiking
MARTHA SQUIRES

Harvard Captain
JEANNETTE BEDARD

Yale Captain
MARGARET O'SHEA

Publicity Director
EVELYN PIKE

Senior Representative
MARIE BUTLER

Junior Representative
WINIFRED MAGER

Sophomore Representative
MOLLY CAREY

Advisers
MISS MIRA WALLACE
MRS. MARGARET KING

W. A. A. Activities

September 6   *Freshmen Orientation*—the choosing of teams, Harvard or Yale. Each girl left spurred on by the motto of the A. A. "A girl for every sport, a sport for every girl, and every girl for a "sport."

October 18   *Harvard-Yale party*—rivalry to extend for four years with competitive games, cheers, and songs. Which team to win the pennant —Harvard or Yale?

November 22   *Pauline Chellis and her dance group*—The New England Suite, The Drill Hour, and the portrait sketch, La Moderne.

January 26   *W. A. A. Semi-formal*—the outstanding social event of the year! The Winter Scenes, the Most Eligible Bachelor, the guestbook— all added to the novelty and enjoyment of the evening.

February 14   *Salem-Bridgewater Basketball Sports Day*—Competition and fun, climaxed by the great Valentine Day storm, and consequent overnight stay, and journey home.

March 14   *Salem-Lowell Basketball Sports Day*—Another day of visiting for play and fun, with both Salem and Lowell reaping two victories.

April 11   *Co-Recreational Sport Nite*—for the first time in the history of our A. A. The Assembly Hall, gym, corridors, and Hygiene room hummed with activity—volleyball, badminton, pingpong, tennekoit, shuffleboard, and dancing; not to forget the hamburgers and coffee.

May 2   *Mock Man Dance*—The Gold Dust Twins, the Dutch Cleanser Lady, Six Delicious Flavors, etc., give you an inkling of our guests. Advertising as the theme with fun and ingenuity prevailing.

May 8   *Modern Dance Recital*—Patterns, techniques, such as leaps and swings, and emotions shown through movements.

May 9   *Modern Dance Symposium at Lowell*—Hardwork reaps its reward in the exchanging of ideas and demonstrating of techniques with the dance groups of Lowell, Fitchburg, Bridgewater, and Framingham.

May 23   *W. A. A. Banquet*—Food, new officers, awards, songs, and sentiment. A farewell to the A. A. for this year and an incentive for the next.

Modern Dance Group

3rd Row: R. Polansky, S. Prescott, E. Pelley, W. Mager, M. Bailey, A. Connick.

2nd Row: R. Reynolds, G. Marques, M. Shosterman, S. Garber, M. Mc-Carty, H. Rovic, E. Sullivan, F. Cirioni.

1st Row: N. Carpinoni, R. Vernick, A. Rentoumis, H. Brownrigg.

Girls' Sports

M. A. A. Executive Board

2nd Row: J. Forte. J. Donegan, C. Santilli. S. Finkle, F. Lipman.
1st Row: E. Thistle, A. Conlon, President; Mr. Lowrey, J. McKinlay, Vice-President; H. Brenner, Secretary.

President
ALBERT CONLON

Vice-President
JAMES McKINLAY

Secretary
HERBERT BRENNER

Treasurer
MAURICE SMITH

Senior Representative
JOHN DONEGAN

Junior Representative
DANIEL PARKS

Sophomore Representative
CHESTER SANTILLI

Freshmen Representative
EVERETT THISTLE

Basketball Captain
SAMUEL FINKLE

Basketball Manager
RICHARD SHEEHAN

Baseball Captains
JOSEPH FORTE
HERBERT BRENNER

Baseball Manager
FREDERIC LIPMAN

M. A. A. Activities

Sept. - June   A diversified athletic and social program provided opportunity for all-round development. The scope of the sports program was successfully enlarged by competition with larger New England colleges.

BASKETBALL

December 15   Gorham Dinner-Dance—The reappearance of Mike Parabolis after a two-year absence.

December 15-   New England Teachers College Basketball Conference. Under
March 13   the spirited leadership of Coach Lowry the team finished with four wins and four losses.

January 19   St. Anselm Game—The first appearance of the Salem Basketeers in flashy brown and orange jackets.

February 7   Bridgewater Game—Who can forget that evening when our jubilant team returned—the first Salem team to beat Bridgewater in its own gym?

March 4   Fitchburg Game—A hard-fought battle for the benefit of the Finnish Relief Fund.

April   Inter-Class Basketball Tournament—Plenty of action and thrills, as well as an opportunity for the underclassmen to display perhaps unsuspected abilities under the watchful eye of the coach.

BASEBALL

April 26   Salem 5   Bridgewater 4
Michael Gradone held Bridgewater to three hits while his mates pounded two opposing hurlers for five runs. Brenner led the attack with a triple and and a single, while Forte drove in two runs and scored two more.

May 3   Salem 3   Gorham 2
Michael Gradone helped himself to his second victory in as many starts by holding the stubborn Maine team to five hits. This game featured brilliant fielding by third-baseman Ray Viens and right-fielder Francis Gilmore.

May 9   New Britain 11   Salem 2
The silver lining of this dark cloud consisted in the fine relief pitching of Dick Clancy, the clutch triple of Joe Forte, and the spectacular baserunning of Ray Viens.

June   The basketball team suffered the loss of six seniors. Captain Samuel Finkle, sharpshooting forward who has held his position for four years, will be missed in the forward court. It will be hard to replace Joe Sullivan, the "fightingest" center in the conference, and high-scoring Herb Brenner. Barney Mazonson, Joe Forte, and George Zoulias will also be greatly missed.
The graduation of four veterans, Co-Captains Joseph Forte and Herbert Brenner, Francis Gilmore, and George Zoulias, gives the baseball team a serious problem to solve next year.

Basketball Team

3rd Row: B. Mazonson, H. Brenner, T. Reddy, J. Sullivan.
2nd Row: G. Zoulias, H. Wall, H. Shumrak, J Forte.
1st Row: Mr. Lowry, S. Finkle, captain; J. Constantinidis.

Baseball Team

2nd Row: W. Stanton, W. Fine, J. Howard, H. Brenner, co-captain; M. Chornesky, M. Gradone, R. Clancy, F. Lipman.
1st Row: G. Zoulias, J. Forte, co-captain; J. Capone, R. Viens, F. Gilmore, T. Reddy.

Directories

Commercial Juniors

BLOOD, LILLIAN	*6 Russell Street, Everett*
BROWN, BERTHA	*14 Shepard Place, Lynn*
CARAN, MILDRED J.	*137 Midland Street, Lowell*
CARPINONE, ANTOINETTA . . .	*14 Freeman Street, Haverhill*
CARROLL, DOROTHY	*23 Harwood Street, Lynn*
CIRIONI, FLORENCE	*183 Mendor Street, Hopedale*
COLOCOUSIS, BESSIE	*1 Arch Avenue, Haverhill*
CONNICK, ALICE	*19 Rollin Terrace, Lynn*
CONSTANTINIDIS, JOHN . . .	*239 School Street, Lowell*
DEVINE, HELEN	*119 Hudson Street, Somerville*
EYNON, EVELYN	*14 Fenton Avenue, Lynn*
EYNON, RUTH	*14 Fenton Avenue, Lynn*
FISCHER, DORIS	*12 Styles Street, Lynn*
FOLAN, EDNA	*27 Plympton Street, Woburn*
FOLEY, ELIZABETH . . .	*48 Woodruff Avenue, Medford*
GARBER, SYLVIA	*15 Commercial Street, Lynn*
GIBBS, WILLIAM	*2 Buchanan Road, Salem*
HEINO, AUNE	*360 Princeton Street, East Boston*
HILL, LOUISE	*65 Center Street, East Weymouth*
HOURIHAN, BERNICE . . .	*12 Jacobs Street, Peabody*
JOHNSON, VIRGINIA . . .	*54 Whittier Street, Lynn*
KAVANAGH, MILDRED . . .	*49 Poplar Street, Danvers*
LEVIN, ELEANOR	*16 Gardner Street, Salem*
MADIAN, CLARA	*334 Broadway, Haverhill*
MAGER, WINIFRED . . .	*209 Prospect Street, Leominster*
MARQUES, GILDA	*55 Spring Street, Stoneham*
MCGARAHAN, MARY . . .	*259 School Street, Lowell*
MOREY, GEORGE	*15 A Taylor Street, Gloucester*
NELSON, EVELYN . . .	*17 High Street, Lynn*
PAPPADOPOULOS, EVANGELOS .	*195 Cross Street, Lowell*
PELLEY, EVA	*14 Smith Street, Lynn*
POLANSKY, RHODA S. . .	*71 Hawthorne Street, Salem*
RENTOUMIS, ATHENA . . .	*24 Foster Street, Salem*
REYNOLDS, RUTH . . .	*Jarvis Avenue, Holyoke*
SHAW, MARJORIE . . .	*Turnpike Road, Billerica*
SHEA, HELENA	*18 Swampscott Avenue, Peabody*
SHOSTERMAN, MARYE . . .	*924 Washington Street, Lynn*
SHUMRAK, HAROLD L. . .	*36 Crosby Street, Lynn*
SIMPSON, BARBARA E. . .	*101 Bonney Street, New Bedford*
SMYRNIOS, PHILIP . . .	*35 Highland Park, Peabody*
SPOFFORD, GRACE . . .	*991 Main Street, Haverhill*
STANLEY, MARJORIE . . .	*35 Reservoir Street, Lawrence*
TARBOX, MARIAN . . .	*11 Sanderson Avenue, East Lynn*

173

Junior High Juniors

Anzuoni, Louise	*150 Turnpike Road, Ipswich*
Attridge, James	*15 Cross Street, Salem*
Beaucage, Robert	*16 Eighth Avenue, Haverhill*
Chase, Eleanor	*479 Essex Street, Lynn*
Clancy, Richard	*22 Fayette Street, Beverly*
Colbert, William	*17 Chester Street, Malden*
Fossa, Mary	*14 Wenham Street, Danvers*
Herlihy, Jane	*58 Highland Avenue, Salem*
Holbrook, Muriel	*69 Lincoln Avenue, Saugus*
Holloran, Julie	*10 Baker Street, Gloucester*
Hughes, Helen	*71 Almont Street, Medford*
Malik, Geneva	*593 Summer Street, Lynn*
Martin, Helen	*188 Fells Avenue, Medford*
McCarthy, Margaret	*35 Simpson Avenue, West Somerville*
McMullen, Rita	*9 Court Street, Medford*
O'Leary, Kathleen	*7 Warner Street, Salem*
Parks, Daniel	*36 Harbor Terrace, Gloucester*
Pirie, Elizabeth	*18 Hardy Road, Swampscott*
Preston, Jane	*18 Forest Avenue, Salem*
Seigal, Joseph	*84 Addison Street, Chelsea*
Sheehan, Richard	*68A Cedar Street, Malden*
Smith, Maurice	*173 Lafayette Street, Salem*
Tedeschi, Edward	*56 Clewly Road, Medford*
Thompson, Miriam	*Archelaus Place, West Newbury*
Waldron, Lurana	*17 Chestnut Street, Beverly*
Witham, Virginia	*31 Waitt Park, Franklin Park, N. Revere*

Alba, Mary	105 Cummings Avenue, Revere
Bergman, Esther	55 Pine Street, Stoneham
Blanchard, Thelma	33 Gordon Street, West Somerville
Boyle, Grace	68 Central Avenue, Revere
Canter, Nina	48 Essex Street, Salem
Cardinal, Mary	6 Court Street, Woburn
Dickson, Ethel	163 Main Street, Amesbury
Flynn, Lorraine	104 Suffolk Street, Chelsea
Forbes, Margaret	76 Greenwood Avenue, Swampscott
Gagnon, Irene	19 Atlantic Avenue, Marblehead
Gallant, Claire	36 Hudson Street, Lynn
Hayman, Miriam	Haverhill Street, Rowley
Horgan, Mary	34 Reynolds Avenue, Chelsea
Houston, Helen	27 Lovett Street, Beverly
Johnson, Eleanor S.	121 Henry Avenue, Lynn
Johnson, Eleanor V.	339 Park Avenue, Revere
Johnson, Phyllis	100 Bellevue Avenue, Melrose
Kay, Virginia	216 Summer Street, Malden
LeClerc, Helen	148 Walnut Street, Brookline
Lobacz, Stella	161 Salem Street, Wakefield
Locke, Miriam	54 Heard Street, Chelsea
Lyons, Dorothea	11 Fremont Street, Malden
MacLellan, Josephine	Main Street, Tewksbury
Magee, Eleanor	154 Beach Street, Revere
McAuliffe, Mary	208 Clifton Street, Malden
O'Shea, Margaret	559 Eastern Avenue, Lynn
Packard, Virginia	10 State Road, Revere
Parks, Barbara	85 Gordon Street, West Somerville
Pike, Evelyn	17 Library Street, Chelsea
Pitts, Phyllis	11 Addison Street, Chelsea
Preston, Rosamond	246 Essex Street, Beverly
Quimby, Althea	82 Main Street, Essex
Riley, Annabella	33 Putnam Road, Revere
Rovic, Helen	430 Broadway, Cambridge
Ryan, Eleanor	15 Kosciusko Street, Peabody
Shaughnessy, Barbara	21 Chester Street, Malden
Shepherd, Eva	13 Stevens Street, Peabody
Squires, Martha	28 Woodlawn Avenue, Everett
Taylor, Virginia	16 Lennox Street, Beverly
Timms, Alice	39 East Newton Street, Boston
Wallace, Marian	42 Endicott Avenue, Revere
Weinstein, Eleanor	26 Prospect Street, Lynn

ALLEN, PHYLLIS G.	4 Oak Street, Whitinsville
ALVEZI, CAROLYN M.	Dock Street, Sandwich
ANDERBERG, ALICE H.	6 Houston Street, Lynn
BALL, VERNELLE	657 Western Avenue, Lynn
BEDARD, JEANNETTE E.	404½ Jefferson Avenue, Salem
BROWN, MARY F.	41 St. Gregory Street, Dorchester
BURKE, ELIZABETH H.	Forestdale
CHORNESKY, MAURICE	16 Arlington Street, Lynn
COFFEY, HELEN L.	Coffin Street, West Newbury
COOPER, GRACE M.	116 Fourth Street, Chelsea
COSTELLO, MARGARET G.	50 West Chestnut Street, Wakefield
D'AMBROSIO, OLYMPIA	16 Bancroft Avenue, Wakefield
DESMOND, JOSEPHINE C.	7 Duxbury Road, Mattapan
DONOVAN, ELIZABETH F.	202 Market Street, Brighton
EGAN, RUTH I.	17 Jefferson Street, Lynn
FINN, MARY A.	10 Cedar Street, Roxbury
GARBER, NANCY L.	27 Harwood Street, Lynn
GODFREY, PEARL M.	160 Chelmsford Street, Lowell
GRADONE, MICHAEL B., JR.	44 West Street, Medford
GERRIG, GLADYS	284 Chestnut Street, Chelsea
HALLETT, CORINNE E.	326 Bolivar Street, Canton
HASSETT, JOAN A.	29 Benton Avenue, Great Barrington
HERMAN, MAURICE L.	179 Franklin Avenue, Chelsea
HYMANSON, NATHAN	25 Blossom Street, Lynn
LANE, JOHN EMBURY	38 South Street, Rockport
LYNCH, NORMAN P.	22 Glendale Street, Dorchester
O'LEARY, JOSEPH	98 Elm Street, Charlestown
STANTON, WILLIAM R.	3 Henry Street, Haverhill
VIENS, RAYMOND J.	33 Broadway, Haverhill
WALL, HENRY L.	79 Park Street, Lynn

Commercial Sophomore II

HARKINS, BARBARA J. .   . . . *11 Savoy Road, Salem*
HUGHES, BARBARA E. .   . . . *57 Clinton Street, Fitchburg*
HUTTULA, LYDIA M. .   . . . *13 Omena Street, Fitchburg*
JANES, RUTH   . . . . *293 Maple Street, Danvers*
JOHNSON, ELSIE A. .   . . . *105 Agawam Street, Lowell*
KELLEY, RITA F.   . . . . *32 Ridgeway Road, Medford*
KENNIS, FRANCES A. .   . . . *54 King Street, Lawrence*
KEYES, RUTH G.   . . . . *50 Pine Street, Lowell*
LOGAN, SANDRA .   . . . . *11 Bellevue Road, Lynn*
LoPORTO, THERESA B.   . . . *123 Washington Avenue, Chelsea*
McKENNA, MADELINE A. .   . . . *530 Pleasant Street, Holyoke*
PINDER, M. ELIZABETH   . . . *203 Lexington Street, East Boston*
QUIGG, SALLY MARY .   . . . *41 Bartlett Street, Charlestown*
REYNOLDS, NORMA K. ·   . . . *10 Court Street, Newburyport*
RICCIARDELLO, LOUISE C.   . . . *253 Paris Street, East Boston*
SAKRISON, DORIS E. .   . . . *182 Linwood Street, Lynn*
SEYMOUR, FRANCES A.   . . . *114 Myrtle Street, Lynn*
SLATTERY, ESTHER J. .   . . . *15 Gardner Street, Beverly*
SMITH, PAULINE W. .   . . . *8 Mill Street, Charlestown*
SIEVE, LILLIAN .   . . . . *15 Rockaway Street, Lynn*
SULLIVAN, CHARLOTTE E. .   . . . *90 Aberdeen Avenue, Cambridge*
TWOMEY, MARY ALICE   . . . *16 Amory Street, Lynn*
WAGNER, VIRGINIA .   . . . *56 Winter Street, Fall River*
WATSON, MARY L. .   . . . *41 Harvest Street, East Lynn*
WEINERMAN, BEATRICE   . . . *7 Jennings Street, Lawrence*
WOOD, MARY I. .   . . . *78 Hampshire Street, Lowell*
ZACCONE, ROSE C.   . . . . *17 Salem Street, Charlestown*
ZEPPERNICK, EDNA I. .   . . . *5 Lincoln Street, Winthrop*

Sophomore I

ABELSON, LILLIAN	34 *West Selden Street, Mattapan*
BOYCE, RALPH G.	145 *Walker Road, Swampscott*
BROWNRIGG, HELEN R.	15 *Kimball Street, Cambridge*
CHRISOMALIS, HELEN	41 *Sagamore Street, Lynn*
CROCKWELL, CHARLES L.	75 *Wicklow Avenue, Medford*
DeSIMONE, ROSE M.	16 *Suffolk Court, Lynn*
DONAHUE, PATRICIA	15 *Hazel Street, Haverhill*
FOLAN, MARY M.	213 *Harvard Street, Cambridge*
GALLANT, A. RUTH	36 *Hudson Street, Lynn*
GILHOOLY, MARY J.	12 *Harvard Street, Somerville*
HILL, M. RUTH	101 *Almont Street, Winthrop*
McKEEMAN, GORDON B.	49 *Burrill Avenue, East Lynn*
McLELLAN, MARY I.	35 *Mystic Street, Everett*
MROSE, IRENE C.	42 *Prosper Street, Malden*
NISSENBAUM, MATHILDA	8 *Hanson Avenue, Somerville*
O'SHEA, HELEN G.	559 *Eastern Avenue, Lynn*
POOLER, ELEANOR	9 *Williams Street, Salem*
RICE, VERA	155 *Union Street, Everett*
SANTILLI, CHESTER W.	15 *Montrose Street, Everett*
SEIGAL, MORRIS	84 *Addison Street, Chelsea*
SULLIVAN, EDNA C.	1 *Hollis Park, Cambridge*
SULLIVAN, MARIE A.	5 *Hood Terrace, Danvers*
TEIXEIRA, MARIE E.	23 *Chipman Street, Dorchester*
THANOS, EVA	31 *Summer Street, Gloucester*
TRAQUAIR, MARGARET G.	231 *North Forest Street, Melrose*
WALSH, MARGARET R.	28 *Willow Street, Cambridge*

Sophomore II

BATCHELDER, LOIS	*18 Cottage Avenue, Winthrop*
CARNEY, RITA M.	*36½ Lynn Street, Peabody*
CONNORS, MARY E.	*18 Hampshire Street, Danvers*
DePAOLO, ELENA J.	*Hillcrest Road, Danvers*
DRISCOLL, ANDREA	*101 Glen Street, Somerville*
FOLEY, GERTRUDE M.	*81 Falcon Street, East Boston*
GAGNON, LOUISE	*13 Pratt Avenue, Beverly*
GALLAGHER, HELEN	*18 Sycamore Street, Somerville*
GREEN, VIRGINIA H.	*10 Lambert Avenue, East Lynn*
HYDE, MARGARET E.	*75 Hillside Avenue, Melrose*
KARP, BESSIE	*39 Leach Street, Salem*
KILEY, MARY C.	*153 Court Road, Winthrop*
LINDEN, VIRGINIA M.	*9 Hillcrest Circle, Swampscott*
LITVACK, EDITH B.	*10 Nichols Avenue, Lynn*
LOMBARD, URSULA M.	*Little Neck Road, Ipswich*
MARR, MARGARET J. K.	*51 High Street, Rockport*
MORANDI, NORMA M.	*22 Austin Street, Somerville*
MURPHY, BEATRIX A.	*9 Central Avenue, Danvers*
MYERS, MILDRED E.	*145 Cottage Street, Chelsea*
PAOLI, ANNIE C. J.	*80 Claremont Avenue, Arlington Heights*
PHELAN, EILEEN F.	*64 Mason Street, Salem*
ROSE, ELEANOR M.	*149 Lowell Street, Somerville*
SACK, RUTH A.	*79 Beacon Hill Avenue, Lynn*

Sophomore III

BAILEY, GERTRUDE B.	28 Winter Street, Medford
BAILEY, MILDRED L.	86 Park Street, West Lynn
BERNSTEIN, MYER	61 Addison Street, Chelsea
CASHMAN, MARY J.	59 Kent Street, Newburyport
COGSWELL, RUTH E.	Cedar Street, Wenham
CAREY, MARION R.	3 Shepard Street, Marblehead
CLOON, ARLINE E.	429 Eastern Avenue, Lynn
CONNOLLY, CATHERINE L.	98 Boston Street, Salem
DALTON, WILLIAM	150 Hale Street, Beverly
DANDENEAU, MARY	731 Chestnut Street, North Andover
FARGO, MARYALICE	15 Hatch Road, Medford
FARRELL, FRANCES T.	9 Whittier Avenue, Amesbury
FLYNN, ELAINE	925 Humphrey Street, Swampscott
FRIEDMAN, BERNICE	26 Sherman Street, Beverly
HAVERTY, MARJORIE	27 Essex Street, Salem
HOWARD, JOHN C.	22 Hurlcroft Avenue, Medford
LOCKE, HERBERT	54 Heard Street, Chelsea
MAEL, MILDRED E.	Millis
MELVILLE, CATHERINE	28 Lowell Street, Lynn
MOODY, BARBARA	3 Sheridan Road, Swampscott
McNEIL, ANNE FRANCES	104 Linden Street, Salem
O'HALLORAN, MARY C.	17 Cedar Cliff Terrace, Medford
NEWELL, LAWRENCE	37 West Street, Malden
REDDY, THOMAS	25 School Street, Salem
SENGER, IRENE	13 Vineyard Street, Danvers
STAPLES, BARBARA	18 Western Avenue, Beverly
STACEY, GRACE	114 Antrim Street, Cambridge

Ahern, Regina M.	52 Wyman Terrace, Arlington
Alpers, Harriet R.	22 Summitt Avenue, Salem
Barry, Robert E.	16 Wickfield Court, Everett
Blacker, Lillian G.	55 Brookledge Street, Roxbury
Cantalupi, Mary R.	82 Bradford Street, Everett
Conlon, Charles R.	5 Morrill Place, Lynn
Cummings, Helen P.	55 Avalon Road, West Roxbury
Dulgarian, Lucy	Woodbine Court, Chelmsford
Fischer, Constance	3 Holly Street, Salem
Flanders, Olive	Spring Street, Vineyard Haven
Frame, Dorothy F.	195 North Street, Salem
Freedland, Estelle	203 Shirley Street, Winthrop
Guidara, Nicholas	19 Astor Street, Lynn
Hajinlian, Rosa	60 Addison Street, Chelsea
Hancock, Joseph H.	30 Boston Avenue, Somerville
Hederson, Helen M.	45 Crescent Avenue, Chelsea
Kierce, Mary E.	98 Cosgrove Street, Lowell
Klubock, Ann T.	163 Dawes Street, Lawrence
Langford, Mary C.	1017 Washington Street, Lynn
Latorella, Angela J.	18 Josephine Street, Dorchester
Lenihan, Madeline R.	11 Wesley Street, Somerville
Machaj, Victoria A.	21 Estes Street, Ipswich
McElaney, Mary M.	34 Washington Street, Charlestown
McGlynn, C. Priscilla	88 McKay Street, Beverly
McKenney, Gladys A.	55 Autumn Street, Lynn
Murray, Eugene I.	26 Gibbens Street, Somerville
O'Neil, Claire	160 Rimmon Avenue, Chicopee
O'Neli, Virginia G.	22 Vista Street, Malden
O'Shea, John P.	12 Fuller Street, Lynn
Palefsky, Shirley	92 Gates Street, Lowell
Pekin, Anita	55 Linden Street, Salem
Pinesult, John L., Jr.	145 Fort Avenue, Salem
Ribaudo, Vincent J.	211 Princeton Street, East Boston
Roberts, Paul N.	61 Ashland Street, Newburyport
Sharp, Irene M. L.	74 Green Street, Charlestown
Shoyo, Mary T.	173 Andover Street, Lawrence
Sloan, Priscilla F.	2 Commonwealth Avenue, Gloucester
Sullivan, Barbara R.	12 Campo Seco Street, Lawrence
Sullivan, Mary E.	800 Locust Street, Fall River
Tenenbaum, Edward	12 Lafayette Park, Lynn
Thomas, Helen	18 Geneva Street, Salem
Thompson, Evelyn E.	51 Winthrop Avenue, Lawrence
Toggerson, Ruth B.	22 Collins Street, Amesbury
Welch, William H.	29 Porter Street, Beverly

BIDDELL, RICHARD G. . . . *19 Wheelwright Road, West Medford*
BUCKLEY, MARGARET M. . . . *17 Mt. Vernon Street, Somerville*
CAPONE, JOHN D. . . . *15 South Cambridge Street, Revere*
CARBONE, MARGUERITE T. . . . *47 Waite Street, Revere*
CLARKIN, EILEEN P. . . . *151 Bridge Street, Salem*
CONNORS, MARY J. . . . *5 Howland Street, Cambridge*
CONWAY, MARIE L. . . . *30 Andrew Street, Salem*
DALEY, JOSEPH F. . . . *107 Bartlett Street, Somerville*
DEWING, NORMA M. . . . *42 Mansfield Road, Lynnfield*
DONOVAN, HOWARD L. . . . *7 Long's Court, Amesbury*
FLIEGEL, NORRIS E. . . . *39 Front Street, Beverly*
FLYGARE, DOROTHY B. . . . *312 Main Street, Gloucester*
FRASER, RALPH S. . . . *10 Kinsman's Court, Ipswich*
HOSKER, FRANCIS M. . . . *8 Warren Street, Lynn*
KELLEY, CARROLL W. . . . *77 Green Street, Lynn*
KIMBALL, AILEEN E. . . . *39 Gage Street, Lynn*
LOSPENNATO, LEDO . . . *58 Prospect Avenue, Revere*
MATTOS, ELEANOR A. . . . *6 Abbott Road, Gloucester*
McRAE, GORDON J. . . . *52 Maple Street, South Hamilton*
MURANO, RAYMOND S. . . . *82 Fifth Street, Chelsea*
MURRAY, JEAN M. . . . *31 Grant Road, Swampscott*
PLANT, DORIS M. . . . *281 Highland Avenue, Somerville*
SAROTA, MOLLY . . . *26 Garland Street, Lynn*
SCOPA, CLAMENTIA L. . . . *359 Boston Avenue, Medford*
SHORE, HELEN . . . *18 Walden Street, Revere*
SILVER, MYER . . . *24 Florence Avenue, Revere*
SLAVIT, SAUL B. . . . *88 Maverick Street, Chelsea*
SWEENEY, JULIA A. . . . *27 Johnson Street, Newburyport*
THISTLE, EVERETT G. . . . *192 Springvale Avenue, Everett*
WEIL, MARGARET M. . . . *19 Cottage Avenue, West Somerville*

Freshman II

BIGGAR, HELEN L.	18 Lancaster Avenue, Revere
CILLIS, HELEN F.	432 Revere Street, Winthrop
CYBUCH, FRANCES	50 Nahant Avenue, Revere
DALAKLIS, MARY	52 Linwood Street, Somerville
DOANE, DORIS	21 Nicholson Street, Marblehead
DONOVAN, ALICE M.	54 Flint Street, Salem
DORON, BLANCHE M.	58 Essex Street, Salem
EASTMAN, DOROTHY H.	2 Pleasant Street, Danvers
EDWARDS, MARJORIE C.	85 Fern Road, Medford
GAGNON, MILDRED I.	School Street, Salisbury
GLASS, MURIEL J.	12 Michigan Avenue, Lynn
HALEY, PATRICIA A.	24 Quincy Street, Malden
HANKINS, SILVIE M.	86 Waverly Street, Everett
HARDING, DOROTHY F.	12 Beach Street, Revere
HYLAND, GLADYS E.	22 Pickett Street, Beverly
JACKSON, ELIZABETH M.	64 Park Street, Danvers
KELLEY, RUTH B.	36 Rand Street, Lynn
LANDER, EVELYN	34 Hancock Street, Salem
LANDINI, YVONNE L.	15 Greenwood Terrace, Somerville
LOVETT, MARY F.	594 Cabot Street, Beverly
MacGREGOR, BETH	3 Elsie Street, Malden
MacINNES, BARBARA E.	31 Read Street, Winthrop
McKAY, JEAN C.	East Orchard Street ,Marblehead
McKERRALL, KATHERINE M.	41 Marie Avenue, Everett
MILTON, ELLA M.	18 Union Street, Newburyport
MIRALDI, MARY	14 Mohan Street, Everett
MULLIGAN, MARGARET A.	21 Sea View Avenue, Revere
NESTOR, ELIZABETH	44 Ridgeway Road, Medford
O'BRIEN, ELIZABETH	75 Beacon Street, Chelsea
PACIFICI, ELVIRA E.	77 Sycamore Street, Somerville
PAQUETTE, ELEANOR M.	15 Fifteenth Avenue, Haverhill
RING, SHIRLEY	164 Allston Street, Allston

Freshman III

AYLWARD, ALICE L.	1117 Saratoga St., Orient Hts., E. Boston
BLUESTEIN, MARION H.	54 Newton Street, Malden
BURWEN, ALTA M.	10 Hazelmere Road, Roslindale
BUSHER, HELEN B.	33 Bromfield Road, West Somerville
CICCARELLI, MARY T.	6 Lexington Street, Everett
DORR, MILDRED	19 North Street, Haverhill
DURANT, VIRGINIA	28 Benton Road, Somerville
FAHEY, ELEANOR	10 Blaisdell Terrace, Lynn
FLAHERTY, BARBARA	20 Baker Road, Everett
FRANCIS, LENA	Gifford Road, Westport
GALLANT, ROBERT A.	9 Olive Street, Revere
GAYTON, ELECTA	588 Second Street, Everett
HENDERSON, SHIRLEY J.	114 Oxford Avenue, Ward Hill
JOYCE, RUTH T.	22 Highland Street, Wakefield
KEEGAN, MARIE E.	91 Boxford Street, Lawrence
LAPPAS, CHARLES	7 Tracey Street, Peabody
MACGILLIVRAY, KATHERINE C.	14 Auburn Street, Wakefield
MALONEY, EDWARD W.	31 Wave Avenue, Wakefield
MACDONALD, MARGARET E.	134 Heath Street, Somerville
O'BRIEN, JEAN	48 River Street, Arlington
O'NEIL, DANIEL	1 Lexington Square, East Boston
ROGERS, RUTH L.	344 Maple Street, Lynn
RAGOZZINA, JOSEPHINE	9 Willard Avenue, Medford
SAXE, SYLVIA	83 Boylston Street, Malden
SCALERA, CARMINE M.	20 Cantillian Street, Lawrence
SMITH, NATALIE I.	50 Gertrude Street, East Lynn
STATES, WINNIFRED M.	80 Windsor Street, Boston
THURLOW, BARBARA E.	528 Maple Street, Hathorne
WELCH, FRANCES A.	921 Broadway, Somerville
WELCH, MARION	127 Josephine Avenue, Somerville
ZETES, CHRISTIE N.	185 Franklin Street, Lynn

CLASS RINGS

PRIZE TROPHIES

PARTY FAVORS

AND

GIFTS FOR EVERY OCCASION

DANIEL LOW'S

IN SALEM

TOMORROW'S BUSINESSMEN

Will Be Trained by You!

Many of our most able college graduates enter commercial teaching because they find it highly interesting work and among the most remunerative of the teaching psitions. We invite all teachers who are going into commercial teaching to make use of of our free services. A letter to one of our offices asking for counsel as to methods, standards, outcomes, or textbook materials will bring an immediate response and will bring a Gregg counsellor to see you on your first job, if you wish. *We try to give every possible service to beginning commercial teachers.*

The Gregg Publishing Company publishes a wealth of textbooks and work materials for use in commercial classes. Among these are Gregg Shorthand, Gregg Typing, Typewriting for Personal Use, and texts in secretarial and office practice, junior business training, economic geography, bookkeeping and accounting, business arithmetic, business English and correspondence, business law, economics, and salesmanship. Supplementing these are commercial teacher magazines and teaching methods books. There is an up-to-date, authoritative Gregg text for every phase of commercial education.

Teachers who use any of these materials are supplied with teacher's manuals and other teaching aids, without charge. Gregg service is designed to help you make a success of commercial teaching. Before going on your first commercial teaching job, write to our nearest office for classified list of Gregg publications.

THE GREGG PUBLISHING COMPANY

NEW YORK - CHICAGO - SAN FRANCISCO - BOSTON
TORONTO - LONDON - SYDNEY

Another Publication...

SHOWING

SARGENT

SUPERIORITY

Complete Photographic Service

to the

1940 Clipper

SARGENT STUDIO, Inc.

BOSTON, MASS.

CPSIA information can be obtained
at www.ICGtesting.com
Printed in the USA
BVHW04*1011190918
527934BV00014B/794/P